GRAND CAN

The tomb or crypt in
found is one of the la:
walls slanting back at an angle of about 35 degrees.
On these are tiers of mummies, each one
occupying a separate hewn shelf. At the head of
each is a small bench, on which is found copper
cups and pieces of broken swords. Some of the
mummies are covered with clay, and all are
wrapped in a dark fabric.

Upwards of 50,000 people could have lived in
the caverns comfortably. One theory is that the
present Indian tribes found in Arizona are
descendants of the serfs or slaves of the people
which inhabited the cave. Undoubtedly a good
many thousands of years before the Christian era,
a people lived here which reached a high stage of
civilization.

One thing I have not spoken of, may be of
interest. There is one chamber of the passageway
to which is not ventilated, and when we approached
it a deadly, snaky smell struck us. Our light would
not penetrate the gloom, and until stronger ones
are available we will not know what the chamber
contains. Some say snakes, but other boo-hoo this
idea and think it may contain a deadly gas or
chemicals used by the ancients.

No sounds are heard, but it smells snaky just the
same. The whole underground installation gives
one of shaky nerves the creeps. The gloom is like
a weight on one's shoulders, and our flashlights and
candles only make the darkness blacker...

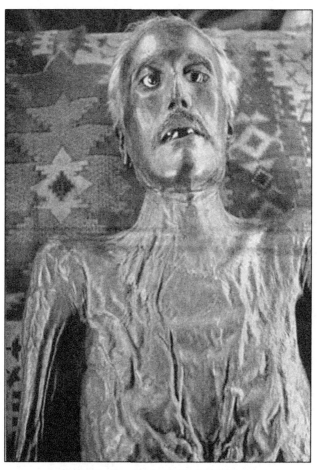

DAVID E. GEORGE MUMMY.

MUMMIES OF THE AMERICAS

Creepy Cadavers, Outlaw Mummies,
and Lost Cities of the Dead

John LeMay

Bicep Books
Roswell, NM

First Edition

LeMay, John.
    Mummies of the Americas: Creepy Cadavers,
Outlaw Mummies, and Lost Cities of the Dead
        1. History—Pioneer Era. 2. Supernatural
        3. Folklore, Early Twentieth Century.

FOR DR. JOHN AND
THE SCARYCAST CREW

PHOTOGRAPHED BY W. J. BOAG, PAWHUSKA, OKLA.

CONTENTS

INTRODUCTION   9

INDEX 191
ABOUT THE AUTHOR 193

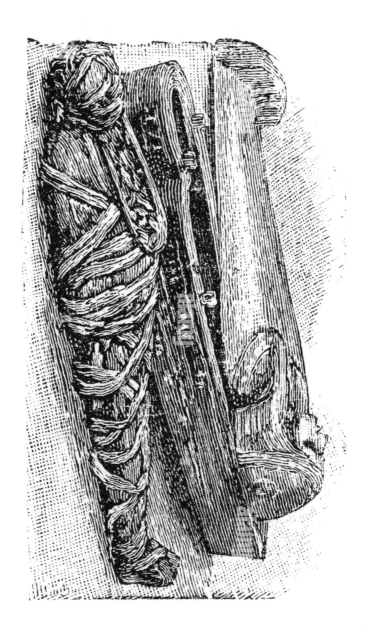

INTRODUCTION:
THE MUMMIES OF EGYPT
(AND HOLLYWOOD)

Our perceptions of mummies come from two very different sources. The first is historical record, of course, and the second is *The Mummy* and its sequels. In 1932, Universal Pictures unleashed Boris Karloff's shuffling mummy, Imhotep. Actually, the title character only appears in the traditional mummy guise in his first scene, and thereafter is a being more akin to Dracula. But, it was the bandaged, shuffling mummy that stood out, and that's what Universal went with in the sequels. And how did they come upon this idea? Both inspirations were historical. The first wasn't Egyptian, though. It was the Italian mystic Cagliostro.

His full name was Count Allesandro Di Cagliostro, and though he wasn't Egyptian, he spent several years in Egypt studying Egyptian mysticism. The enigmatic magician claimed that he was 3,000 years old, among other things, and in 1777 he founded the Egyptian Rite of

Freemasonry. By 1785, his home was ornately decorated with Egyptian symbols and his servants dressed in Egyptian robes. In 1789 he was arrested as part of the Inquisition and thrown in jail where he died... or did he? According to legend, he didn't die as no body was ever found. He simply disappeared from his cell.

ALESSANDRO CAGLIOSTRO (1789) BY DANIEL CHODOWIECKI.

1882 DEPICTION OF CAGLIOSTRO
PERFORMING MAGIC.

A screenwriter at Universal, Nina Wilcox Putnam, was inspired by the idea and wrote a horror thriller called *Cagliostro, King of the Dead.* Over time, Universal became so enamored with the Egyptian aspects of the script that it eventually evolved into *The Mummy* sans any mention of the Italian mystic.

The aspect of the mummy's curse came from the much-sensationalized discovery of King Tut's tomb, of course, which takes us back to the historical record. The Tomb of Tutankhamun was discovered in the Valley of the Kings in November of 1922 by archaeologist Howard Carter and his patron, George Herbert, 5th Earl of Carnarvon. The discovery was so sensational at the time that it even kicked off a trend of Egyptian-inspired design motifs! Things really kicked into high gear in April of 1923 when Herbert died of an infection. He was the first of what would eventually become known as the Curse of King Tut. Sherlock Holmes creator Sir Arthur Conan Doyle even chimed in to suggest that "elementals" created by Tutankhamun's priests to guard the royal tomb were responsible.

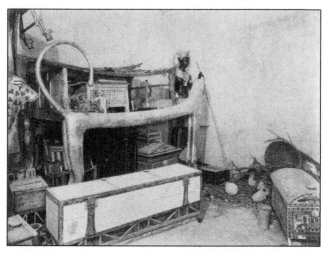

KING TUT'S TOMB C.1922.

Before Herbert's death, another strange incident had occurred. Upon finding the tomb, Carter had sent a messenger to the home of famous Egyptologist James Henry Breasted. As the messenger approached the residence, he claimed to hear a haunting, "faint, almost human cry." Amplifying the sinister atmosphere was a macabre discovery: a pet canary kept at the home was found dead in the jaws of a cobra coiled up within the cage. Perhaps not coincidentally, cobras were synonymous with Egyptian monarchy.[1]

DISCOVERY OF KING TUT'S TOMB C.1922.

This, as it turned out, was an omen for worse things to come, such as the death of Herbert and others. In 1925, a friend of Carter's, Sir Bruce Ingram, suffered a tragic accident when his home burned down. When he had it rebuilt, a flood soon followed, ruining the next house! Previous to this, Carter had gifted Ingram with a mummified hand. On its wrist was a scarab bracelet inscribed with the following: "Cursed be he who moves my body. To him shall come fire, water, and pestilence."

---

[1] Like the cobra that attacked the canary, in 1926, Carter glimpsed another animal associated with the Egyptian dynasty. For the first time ever in his 35 years of working in the Egyptian desert, Carter saw with his own eyes a jackal, which was the basis for Anubis.

Three other men who either visited the tomb or were a part of the excavation also died within a few years of being in the crypt. However, Carter himself didn't pass away until sixteen years later, though some still attributed it to the curse.

Though Egypt is the spot most associated with mummies, mummified bodies of humans and animals are found all over the world. In fact, the oldest one ever was found within Spirit Cave near Fallon, Nevada, in 1940. That's a long way from Egypt. Likewise, not all mummies were ancient, either. Some, like the infamous mummy of a man who claimed to be John Wilkes Booth, were more or less created by accident in the early 1900s and became a roadshow sensation.

It is mummies such as these that this tome endeavors to explore, unearthing them from the sands of North and Central America rather than the faraway Middle East. And though this volume may deviate from the supernatural nature of its two sister tomes—sorry, no reanimated mummies here save for one—a few of the mummies found in this book had curses of their own attributed to them. Whether the "curses" were simply unfortunate coincidences or a North American variant of the Curse of the Pharaohs, they have a fascinating history all their own.

CHAPTER 1
THE GUNSLINGER MUMMY

In the early 1900s, even before the discovery of King Tut's Tomb caused a media sensation, there was a trend in mummified remains being used as sideshow attractions. The most famous of these was undoubtedly the mummy of David E. George, alias John Wilkes Booth, which will be covered in a later chapter. Among the other more famous sideshow mummies were Elmer, the outlaw mummy, and Queho, a Native American mummy from Eldorado, Nevada. And then there's Sylvester.

According to legend, two cowboys stumbled across Sylvester's mummified corpse in Arizona's Gila Bend region around 1895, though more recent data shows that this is likely false. From tests conducted in 2001, it became apparent that the mummy was far too well-preserved to have simply been left out in the desert. In fact, Sylvester—the nickname bestowed upon the unnamed body—is one of the best-preserved mummies of all time.

**SYLVESTER THE MUMMY
AT YE OLDE CURIOSITY SHOPPE.**
[JMABEL, CC BY-SA 3.0 VIA WIKIMEDIA COMMONS]

Experts are certain that an embalmer had to have injected arsenic immediately after "Sylvester's" death. Even Sylvester's tongue was still intact! Why the rush to preserve this Old West John Doe? We don't know, but the mummy was touring the U.S. along with his brethren in the early 20th Century.[2] In 1909, he was spotted at Seattle's Alaska Yukon

---

[2] Supposedly, Sylvester was at least once falsely advertised as the famous John Wilkes Booth mummy.

Exposition. In 1912, he turned up in a Yuma, Arizona, barbershop. By 1915, he was appearing in San Francisco's Panama-Pacific Exposition. And by the 1930s, he was under the care of a doctor who kept him under his couch! Specifically, the doctor had somehow built a couch around a glass display case. Therefore, when the doctor asked his guests to look under the sofa cushion they were about to sit on, they would see the mummy.

Sylvester was procured by the Ye Old Curiosity Shop of Seattle, Washington, for a meager $25 in 1955. Later, the mummy was exhibited at the 1962 Seattle World's fair as a "Desperado from the Old West," though today he's better known as the "Gunslinger Mummy." Unlike many mummies who have become lost over the years, Sylvester has actually remained in Seattle since the 1950s.

As to why Sylvester has been nicknamed "the Gunslinger Mummy," this is because he has a gunshot wound in his chest, implying he "died with his boots on" in the slang of the Wild West. This ties in with yet another uncertain anecdote which claims that before he was Sylvester, the mummy was called McGinty and was the creation of a conman named Soapy Smith. Soapy Smith had a racket wherein he sold bars of soap with money hidden inside them. As hopeful buyers remained optimistic that they'd be the ones to buy the bar with the hidden loot, Soapy always made sure his shills within the crowd got the special bars and the money made its way back to him.

Some say that McGinty/Sylvester was himself a conman, and it was cheating at cards that finally made him catch a bullet. Sylvester stumbled out of whatever saloon he got shot at and made it as far as Gila Bend before bleeding to death. According to this version, the blowing sands dried out and mummified his body overnight. According to more fantastic legends, right after being shot—and this sounds exactly like something out of an old Universal chiller—Sylvester's body was experimented on by a doctor trying out a new embalming technique. And perhaps this really was the case—the doctor at least if not the saloon brawl—since all of Sylvester's internal organs were exceptionally well preserved.

Despite the exquisite preservation of Sylvester's internal organs, the bit about the perennial mad scientist is probably just folklore. Furthermore, modern experts—and don't you just hate them for ruining a good story?—say that the hole in his chest isn't a bullet wound. It was likely made by a drill to mimic a bullet wound, and then red paint was placed around the hole to resemble blood.

However, not all is lost when it comes to Sylvester's mystique. Though he may not have died with his boots on as they say, Sylvester clearly led an adventurous life as shotgun pellets were found in his right cheek, neck, and lungs. As these wounds were non-fatal, the experts are fairly certain Sylvester died of tuberculosis at the age of 45. In life, Sylvester stood 5 feet 11 inches tall and probably weighed 225 pounds, though the corpse today still weighs a hefty 137 pounds.

CHAPTER 2
AZTEC PRINCESS
OF CAPITAN

The subject of lost cities full of wealth and mystery is one that never ceases to grow old. Regardless of the fact that the once mythical jungles of Africa and South America have for the most part been explored, the spacious barren deserts of the Southwest mapped out, and satellite imagery can now pinpoint most anything on Earth, people still refuse to believe that their legendary lost cities do not exist.

Hopes are still high that one day on the ocean floor the real city of Atlantis will be found, the riddles of Easter Island will prove to be remnants of the lost continent of Mu, a forgotten civilization rests somewhere under the frozen ice of Antarctica, and even that somewhere, somehow, the fabled lost kingdom of Cibola, otherwise known as the Seven Cities of Gold, exists waiting to be discovered out in the deserts of the Southwest.

A Scene in the El Capitan Mts, nea

But why, then, if much of the land has been mapped out and explored, do people still believe lost cities of wealth and gold are waiting to be found? To the faithful, the answer is simple: if you can't find them above the ground, then they must be below it.

ar Roswell, N, M.,

This certainly isn't a new concept in works of fiction. The lost city of Atlantis is found underground in the 1957 adaptation of Jules Verne's *Journey to the Center of the Earth,* and more recently, when Nicholas Cage went searching for Cibola in *National Treasure: Book of Secrets* the fabled city was found underground also (of all places behind Mount Rushmore).

In Southeastern New Mexico, an elaborate Aztec treasure city may lie hidden in the Capitan Mountains. The fantastic story begins in the 16th Century during the time of the Spanish conquest of the Aztec Empire in Mexico when Hernan Cortés took Emperor Montezuma prisoner in his own kingdom. At this time, Montezuma instructed a cavalcade of Aztecs to head north towards their mythical homeland of Aztl'an and hide most of their gold. This way the evil invaders could never possess it.

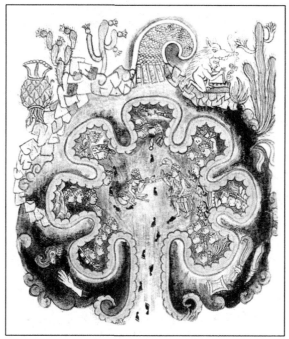

AZTL'AN

"When Cortés held Montezuma captive, the Aztec gave instructions that all Aztec gold be hidden from the Spaniards, so the legend goes and appears to be confirmed by the fact there was nowhere near the gold after the conquest there should have been," says veteran treasure hunter Jack Purcell, who is also the author of the book *The Lost Adams Diggings: Myth, Mystery and Madness.* "The legends say four groups of 1000 Aztecs each carried the treasures to different places in the north and hid them there."[3]

As Purcell stated above, four columns consisting of 1,000 Aztecs set out on their own separate ways to hide their valuables which included hundreds of tons of gold and precious jewels northward. One of the caravans apparently chose a spot in the Capitan Mountains nearby present-day Ruidoso, New Mexico, to hide their gold. Some say the Aztecs knew about this cave beforehand because it was said to have been "hollowed out by a race of giants" that had once lived there.

Once the majestic Capitans were in sight of the nobles in charge of the caravan, they threatened the nearly one thousand slaves in their decree with death if the mountains were not reached by sundown. By the end of the day they would reach the mountains, but in the process, many slaves would perish from exhaustion and some from poisonous snake bites. On the morning of the next day, the Aztecs would find the entrance to this lost cave of giants and make their way inside...

---

[3] Email to the author.

Most of this tale unearthed by treasure hunter Wally Hesse which he related in an old magazine called *Treasure Search*. In the article, Hesse writes:

For seventeen suns they labored, building a small city in this giant cavern. On the eighteenth day, the highest born king flung himself from the high cliff, to meet the gods and declare their wishes had been carried out. That night in the light of the full moon, the queen prepared herself and her two children to offer their hearts to their terrible gods. The stone altar inside the entrance changed slowly from a dull granite grey to a crimson red as the high priest held a large pulsating heart aloft and laid it gently beside the two smaller hearts which were now devoid of all movement.

From then on, the queen and her children's mummified remains have allegedly watched over the doorway to the underground city built by the Aztec slaves. Upon leaving, the priest and the remaining slaves sealed the doorways so that no one else could enter or find the city. The caravan returned to Mexico with the idea that one day, when the Spanish invaders had been driven away, they would come back and reclaim their treasure.

Wally Hesse became aware of this story when he placed an ad in the *Denver Post* stating that he had $1,000 to invest in a "valid mining venture." The most interesting answer Hesse received came from an old man in Roswell, New Mexico, who claimed to have found a lost Aztec treasure cave in the

Capitan Mountains. The old man told Hesse how he had found a cave in the mountains with a flight of stone steps leading down them. However, he could only look into the cave, not descend into it as the opening was too small. The old man was reluctant to dynamite the entrance, which is why he responded to Hesse's ad in the *Denver Post.*

Hesse went down to Roswell with a jeep and some dynamite and the two traveled westward towards the Capitans. The old man's age however prevented him from being able to show Hesse the exact spot, as the land was too hard to traverse for the old timer who had been younger when he first found the cave. "It's right over that ridge, Wally," the old man said to Hesse. "I can't make it. Go locate it. I'll take it slow and head back to camp."

In the vast Capitans, Hesse was unable to find the cave the old man claimed was just over the ridge and decided to go back to camp. The next morning they heard over the radio that a heavy snow was coming and decided to go back home and try again later.

In the time that followed, Hesse kept in touch with the old man and before he died, he told Hesse in greater detail what the formations near the cave opening looked like. Hesse kept researching the old man's claims even after he had died and claims to have found many facts corroborating the old man's story, although he never states in his article just what those facts were.

On a return trip to the area, Hesse said that he found an old poplar tree with carved markings of an Indian in full headgear, a turtle, and an arrow carved into it. It is common knowledge to treasure hunters that turtles often represent treasures. And, the arrow carved into the tree pointed in the same direction the old man claimed the treasure was located. Hesse cut the portion out of the tree and with help from a friend in Ruidoso took it to Eugene Chihuahua, an old Apache man living at the Mescalero Apache Indian Reservation nearby. Chihuahua said that the signs either pointed to treasure, water, or possibly both.

Later Hesse said he found a giant rock formation that bared similarities to a turtle in alignment with where the arrow had pointed. Eventually, Hesse mounted a formal expedition to find the cave entrance with a European Mountain climber, Kurt Richardson, and an English illustrator, Julia Purcell, to map out the rock formations. The trio got close to finding the area on the very last night of the expedition, but with supplies running low, they had to turn back the next morning. Hesse's article ends optimistically stating that one day he plans to return to the site and find the hidden city of the Aztecs once and for all.

Apparently, Hesse never found the treasure, and so far he is the only one to have ever written about it extensively. "It's kind of hard to believe that a legend with hundreds of years of folk to folk mileage would not at the very least hold some truth," says Mickey Cochran, a long time Ruidoso resident and co-owner of Go West Marketing. "I believe even the Lost Dutchman's Mine pales in comparison to the Capitan Treasure Cave both in value and validity. Yet, the Capitan Treasure Cave isn't near as famous ... and, surprisingly, it's quite difficult to find any historical documentation. It's almost as if this treasure's history has been long hidden from the public ... which makes it even more mysterious and intriguing."[4]

UNRELATED STOCK IMAGE OF THE DISCOVERY OF AN AZTEC MUMMY.

Cochran also met someone who had a similar story to Hesse's. "I have personally met someone, back when I worked as an in-house artist for Bounty Hunter Metal Detectors, who claimed with full astuteness, that he had spent half his lifetime looking for this particular cave ... and in the process, had discovered symbols carved in rock that denoted this particular Aztec treasure was in close proximity to where he was hunting. He was in

---

[4] Email to author.

search of a gravitometer at the time ... for he believed that the cave was well buried or maybe even caved in by the Aztecs. Thusly, the only way he would discover this treasure would be via a way to measure gravitational pull with the hopes of revealing cavities in the earth."

Several Roswell residents have also heard similar stories about a cave in the mountains with a series of stone steps descending to an underground city. Jack Purcell has also heard of the lost treasure of the Capitans but remains more skeptical. "I suspect the Capitans story ain't a good one, though I suppose it might be. Maybe the Aztecs had an outpost up there somewhere and were mining on that side of the Rio Grande, also," speculates Purcell.

Does a secret underground Aztec outpost remain in the Capitan Mountains? Only the mountains know for certain, and they aren't telling.

Sources:

Hesse, Wally. "Capitan's Gold." *Treasure Search*, n.d.

CHAPTER 3
THE MUMMY OF HELLDORADO

Starting in 1934, Las Vegas, Nevada, has held a Wild West-themed rodeo once a year called Helldorado Days. It was the invention of Clyde Zerbythe and was organized by the Benevolent and Protective Order of Elks as a fundraiser for local charities. Part of the impetus for the festival was the ongoing construction of Hoover Dam. Having begun construction in 1931, the massive undertaking was nearing its end in 1934, and Las Vegas wanted to lure some of the departing workers into town (as if all the recently constructed casinos weren't enough).

The festival derived its name from the nearby Eldorado Canyon, cleverly nicknamed Helldorado for all the bloodshed there during the Wild West.

Eldorado Canyon was the home of several gold mines and, if you recall, is also haunted by the so-called Hellhounds of Eldorado Canyon covered in *Cowboys & Dogmen.* However, Eldorado was also home to another type of monster, and this one was human. If the accusations are true, this man was Nevada's first mass killer and may have murdered 23 people. His name was Queho, and when his mummified body was discovered in 1940, the Elks decided to use him as an attraction in Helldorado Days.

QUEHO'S REMAINS UNEARTHED C.1940.
(UNLV SPECIAL COLLECTIONS)

To display the Queho mummy, the Elks constructed a nice glass case and then put it in an artificial cave replica of Queho's hideout within Las Vegas's Helldorado Village. On at least one occasion, Queho's mummy even rode in the Helldorado parade (not under its own power, of course). So far as we know, Queho was on exhibition until the early 1950s until he was retired.

Most experts place Queho's birth around the year 1880 at Cottonwood Island near Nelson, Nevada. His mother died shortly after giving birth to him, and the identity of his father is unknown, but some have speculated him either to be a Paiute from a neighboring tribe, a white soldier from Fort Mohave or possibly even a miner from Mexico. Due to his mixed blood, considered taboo at the time, plus an unfortunate club foot, the poor boy was rejected by his tribe.

The historical record states that Queho was raised on a reservation in Las Vegas and went to work as a ranch hand as soon as he was old enough. In addition to that, he also worked as a wood gatherer for several of the mining camps, likely including the ones of Eldorado Canyon.

Due to his being orphaned at a young age and being rejected by his tribe, Queho not surprisingly led a harsh existence that hardened him into a criminal. Supposedly, he committed his first murder, that of another member of his tribe, at the age of 17 in 1897. That was just hearsay, though, and more reputable stories state that it wasn't murder, but tribal justice. When Queho's half-brother, Avote, went on a murderous rampage, it was decreed that Queho be the one to bring him to justice. Queho set out with another man, Jim White, into the labyrinth of canyons winding around the Colorado River and found his brother where he was born on Cottonwood Island.

The incident was recalled in an article in *The Nevadan* in 1966, in which Ray Chesson wrote, "Stalking Avote on the island, Queho and White let the killer pass them in the wash. They shot him from behind, which, as Queho said, seemed the most sensible way to do the job." Rather than dragging the body through the arduous landscape, Queho cut off Avote's hand, which was distinctive in that it lacked one finger, and took it back as proof of the kill.

While that killing was justified under tribal law, the first real murder pinned on Queho was recorded in November of 1920, when he was accused of killing a tribesman, Harry Bismark, in a drunken dispute on the reservation. After this, he allegedly killed two Paiute to obtain their horses and fled the area.

On his way to Nelson, Queho stopped to steal supplies from a Las Vegas store. He was confronted by the shopkeeper, Hy Von, and Queho bashed him over the head with a pick handle and broke both of his arms, though remarkably the man wasn't killed. Instead of making it to Nelson like he planned, Queho instead hid out in Eldorado Canyon.

Shortly after this, Queho came under the employ of a woodcutter named J.M. Woodworth. When Woodworth failed to pay Queho his wages, Queho beat him to death with a piece of timber. A posse was formed under Deputy Sheriff Howe to investigate Woodworth's murder, and it was there that they found a distinctive print showing Queho's clubfoot. They followed the trail back to Eldorado Canyon where they found yet another dead body, that of the Gold Bug Mine watchman L.W. "Doc" Gilbert. Queho had apparently shot him in the back and absconded with his badge. The posse continued pursuit of Queho to the Colorado River, where the trail went cold. Though the men thought that Queho wouldn't get far, and would also be easy to track due to his deformed foot, that wasn't the case.

**PROSPECTORS CAMPING
IN ELDORADO CANYON C.1907.
(UNLV SPECIAL COLLECTIONS)**

The chase resumed later that year under the charge of Nevada State Police Sergeant Newgard, who employed several Native American trackers to aid his search. They found evidence of Queho's presence in the area, but the outlaw eluded capture for so long that the party ran out of supplies and returned to Las Vegas in February of 1911.

THE QUEHO POSSE.

Due to his evasive nature, most of the unsolved killings and thefts in the Eldorado Canyon area were pinned on Queho and his legend increased year by year. Queho was even accused of killing his friend, Canyon Charlie, in 1913. Canyon Charlie was 100 years old, blind, and owned few possessions, so it was doubtful that Queho killed him. As stated before, Canyon Charlie was said to be a friend and confidant of Queho's. Still, years later in 1938, the *Las Vegas Evening Review Journal* wrote that, "Charlie's meager supply of food was gone; mute testimony of the terrifying fact that this ghost-like maniac would kill for anything — or nothing — since he might easily have stolen the old man's belongings without resorting to murder."

Over the years, the bodies kept piling up and Queho kept taking the blame, including two miners shot in the back at Jenny Springs, and a Native American woman killed around the same time.

Eventually, a $2,000 reward was offered for Queho's capture dead or alive. Coincidental or not, the killings died off around this point. However, Queho's reputation had become legend. He was the phantom renegade of the hills, the bogeyman that parents warned their children about, and if ever anyone disappeared for as little as a few hours, they feared that Queho had gotten them.

After a six year absence, the killings resumed in January of 1919 with two dead prospectors identified as William Hancock and Eather Taylor, who were discovered upstream from Eldorado Canyon. As was by now the norm, both men had been shot in the back, and Taylor had the added distinction of having been bashed over the head with an ax handle. Though the last few killings were linked to Queho purely by speculation, this time his trademark footprint was found.

Not long after on January 21ˢᵗ, another killing occurred near the Techatticup Mine in which Queho may have been framed. The official story went that the wife of an Eldorado Canyon miner named Maude Douglas awoke one night to the sounds of someone trying to steal some canned goods from the family cabin. For some reason, it was her rather than her husband who went to investigate and ended up taking a shotgun blast to the chest. Supposedly Queho's distinctive footprints were found yet again. I say supposedly because a little boy in Maude's care claimed that it was the husband who had shot Maude, but no one took him seriously.

After this, the reward for Queho's capture and/or elimination increased to $3,000. More determined than ever, local authorities dictated that the best trackers available be hired to find Queho once and for all. The trail led north through Las Vegas Wash and into the Muddy Mountains, where, once again, it went cold. Still, the trackers spent another two months amidst freezing rain and snow until finally they found something: more dead bodies, in this case two miners who went missing years ago. Queho had evaded capture yet again.

Sightings of the elusive Queho began to become fewer and fewer, and the last recorded one actually took place in February of 1930 when Queho was spotted walking right down Fremont Street in Las Vegas. A policeman recognized the old outlaw and called for reinforcements. It turned out to be Queho's last escape, as he was never seen alive again.

On February 18, 1940, three prospectors found the mummified dead body of a Native American man high up in a cave on the side of Black Canyon. The cave was the perfect hideout for a legendary figure like Queho, being about 2,000 feet above the river and looking down at the canyon. It was rigged with a trip wire which would trigger an alarm bell inside the cave when trespassers came calling. But the men need not have worried. Queho was found curled up in a fetal position, having succumbed after all those years to the bite of a rattlesnake. Along with the body were found a Winchester 30/30 rifle, provisions and items stolen in recent years linked to the construction of Hoover Dam nearby, and a "special deputy badge," the serial number of which matched that of L.W. "Doc" Gilbert killed in 1910. This, along with the corpse's double row of teeth distinctive to Queho, more or less proved that the body had to be Queho's.

**QUEHO'S REMAINS UPON DISCOVERY.
(UNLV SPECIAL COLLECTIONS)**

Frank Wait, the current Chief of Police of Las Vegas and, more importantly, a member of the

1910 posse charged with finding Queho, rushed to identify the body and pronounced it as Queho. The find was announced to the press on February 21st and the papers had a ball with the story. Meanwhile, the body's discoverer, Charles Kenyon, expected to get the long unclaimed reward money for Queho and was denied. As such, he threatened to take back possession of the body from the Palm Funeral Home so that he could sell it to the Las Vegas Elks Club for exhibition purposes, but a court order was issued to prevent this.

CLARKE KENYON, FRANK WAIT AND ART
SCHROEDER WITH QUEHO MUMMY.
(UNLV SPECIAL COLLECTIONS)

Elsewhere, several Native American men came from out of nowhere claiming to be Queho's heirs—highly suspicious since Queho was rejected since birth. Queho's mummified corpse was now essentially the prize in a tug-o-war between the two parties. With wisdom worthy of King Solomon, the Palm Funeral Home suddenly announced that whoever owned the body was also responsible for the bill. The heirs and Kenyon quickly disappeared, and a judge granted the funeral home rights to the body.

Three years later, the funeral home threatened to cremate the mummy and scatter its ashes in the desert if no one stepped forward to claim it and pay for their services! Oddly enough, it was Frank Wait who footed the bill and then donated Queho's remains and artifacts to the same Las Vegas Elks Club that Kenyon had intended to sell them to. As stated in this chapter's introduction, the mummy then became one of the main attractions of Helldorado Days in Las Vegas.

There are conflicting reports as to where Queho ended up next. Some say Queho's mummy made its way to the Museum of Natural History at the University of Nevada, where it was housed until the mid-1970s. Others say Queho's body and artifacts were stolen, and the bones were later found scattered in Bonanza Wash. Whether housed in an institute or strewn about Bonanza Walsh, the bones were eventually acquired by a retired Las Vegas attorney, Roland H. Wiley, in 1975. On November 6th of that year, Nevada's first serial killer, if he could be called that, was finally given a proper burial in the vicinity of Wiley's Pahrump Valley ranch. At the ceremony, Frank Wait told the press that he was relieved to finally see the corpse laid to rest after many years.

In retrospect, some historians have defended Queho since many of the murders pinned on him out of the 23 can't be proven. Some of his kills, according to the hard frontier laws of the time, could be argued as justified, such as the man who never paid Queho the wages owed to him. Furthermore, many accounts that paint Queho in a purely murderous light conveniently skip over stories of prospectors in the region who had peaceful, pleasant encounters with Queho, of which there was a decent amount.

Ray Chesson probably summed it up best in *The Nevadan* when he wrote,

Just how many people Queho killed, and under what circumstances, will probably never be known. During the course of his career, he was accused of practically every murder committed in the vicinity of Eldorado Canyon. ... His story has been hammered and mauled and shaped by writers across the entire spread of America, and Lord only knows where some of them got their material.

Ultimately, at this point, the truth of Queho is unfortunately lost to the sands of time. But one thing is for certain, the man had the odds stacked against him from birth, and justified or not, Queho

QUEHO'S SUPERNATURAL HERITAGE?

Author Cory Daniel of The Phoenix Enigma put forth the unique theory that Queho may have evaded capture for so long thanks to supernatural abilities. And why would he think this, you surely ask? This is because Queho was proven to have a double row of teeth. No simple case of Hyperdontia where a person might have a few extra teeth, Queho had a full double row. Hyperdontia is very rare in of itself at 0.1% to 3.8%, but a complete double row of teeth was something common to accounts of the biblical giants.

These huge beings were the offspring of angels and human women, and in addition to the double rows of teeth also had six digits on their hands and feet rather than the usual five. While Queho had only five digits, the double row of teeth is eyebrow raising, and it was also said that Queho was quite tall. Daniel also speculated that perhaps, if Queho was indeed guilty of all the murders attributed to him, that the ultra-violent tendencies could have stemmed from the lineage of the giants, which were excessively violent. Lastly, he drew a parallel between Queho's remains being exploited by a fraternal society much in the same way that Geronimo's stolen skull is used in ceremonies for the Skull and Bones Society at Yale. (For those unaware, Geronimo himself was said to have supernatural powers, hence the interest in his skull.)

And, before you completely roll your eyes at the theory that Queho was superhuman, his contemporaries, notably the lawmen who failed to capture him, were positively flabbergasted at just how well he evaded capture in such harsh terrain. And naturally, there are those today that claim to occasionally still see Queho stalking the canyons of Eldorado...

became the scapegoat for every ill-deed committed in Eldorado Canyon.

Sources

"Queho." *Las Vegas Review Journal.* (February 7, 1999) https://www.reviewjournal.com/news/queho/

Daniel, Cory. "Queho." Phoenix Enigma.
https://thephoenixenigma.com/queho/

CHAPTER 4

BONFIRE OF THE MUMMIES

Universal's classic Mummy series spanned from 1932 up until 1945, which ended with the Mummy, Kharis, being entombed in the Deep South of North America in *The Mummy's Curse*. Though the South may seem to be an odd region to dig up a mummy, in fact, hundreds of mummies were discovered there in the early 1800s.

The story of Kentucky's mummies was unearthed by Thomas Ashe, an Irish writer and adventurer who was journeying across America in the early 1800s. His discoveries and experiences were preserved in correspondence to a colleague in London.

THOMAS ASHE.

Ashe was particularly interested in ancient
mounds and burial sites. In the summer of 1806,
Ashe was in Lexington, Kentucky, where he heard
of the discovery of an ancient tomb, one that
possibly outdated even the Native American tribes

known to inhabit the region. In his book, *Travels in America*, Ashe wrote:

LEXINGTON, KENTUCKY C.1870s.

Lexington stands nearly on the site of an old Indian town, which must have been of great extent and magnificence, as is amply evinced by the wide range of circumvolutory works, and the quantity of ground it once occupied. Time, and the more destructive ravage of man, have nearly leveled these remains of former greatness with the dust, and would possibly allow them to sink into an entire oblivion, were they not connected with a catacomb, formed in the bowels of the limestone rock, about fifteen feet below the surface of the earth, and lying adjacent to the town of Lexington. This grand object, so novel and extraordinary in America, was discovered about twenty years ago (1786) by some of the first settlers, whose curiosity was excited by something remarkable in the character of stones which struck their attention while hunting in the woods.

They removed the stones, which revealed other stones "of curious workmanship." These they also removed and, while doing so, inadvertently exposed the mouth of a deep, dark cavern of tremendous size. Amazed at their discovery, they gathered more men and a sufficient amount of ropes and torches, then descended into the cave. They found themselves in a "spacious apartment; the sides and extreme ends were formed into niches and compartments, and occupied by figures representing men! When alarm subsided, and the sentiment of dismay and surprise permitted further research and inquiry, the figures were found to be Indian mummies, preserved by the art of embalming to great preservation and perfection of state!"

What made the mummies of such great interest was the fact that Native Americans of the time weren't known to embalm their dead in the manner of the ancient Egyptians. However, the discoverers didn't know that, nor were they concerned with historic preservation in the slightest. At that time, white settlers and Native Americans were in the middle of an all-out war. So much hostility existed between them in the Kentucky region that when the men found what they assumed to be dead Indians, they took to lighting the bodies on fire!

...the discoverers of the catacomb delighted to wreak their vengeance... They dragged the mummies to the day, tore the bandages open, kicked the bodies into dust, and made a general bonfire of the most ancient remains antiquity could boast; of remains respected by many hundred revolving years, held sacred by time, and unsusceptible to corruption, if not visited by profane and violating hands!

Upon hearing of this unfortunate bonfire of the mummies, which literally put America's ancient history up in smoke, Ashe gathered together a group of men to help him find the tomb. They did, and Ashe investigated the cave, finding a large, square-shaped cavern 300-feet-long by 100-feet-wide with a level floor and an eighteen-foot-tall, vaulted ceiling. The vaulted ceiling, more than anything, in addition to the niches and shelves along the wall, proved that this was indeed a man-made crypt, and not a completely naturally formation. He estimated that it may have held upwards of 2,000 mummies. When he asked the locals how many they thought it contained, they answered that the bodies had been "burned by the hundreds."

I can bear testimony to the industry and determination of the curious who resort to it to efface every mark of workmanship, and to destroy every evidence of its intention or original design! The angles and ornaments of the niches are mutilated; all projections and protuberances are struck off; every mummy removed, and so many fires have been made in the place, either to warm visitors or to burn up the remains, that the shades, dispositions, and aspects, have been tortured into essential difference and change."

It seems rather ironic that the ignorant townsfolk burned all the mummies because they assumed they were Native American when, at the same time, they were observant enough to notice that the mummies had red hair! They also seemed to imply that there was almost something supernatural in the way that the bodies burst into flame as they stated that they burned "with a rapidity that baffled all observation and description."

Ultimately, Ashe and his hired hands were only able to collect baskets of scraps and rubbish that survived the fire. Among the scraps were "several pieces of human limbs, and fragments of bodies, solid, sound and apparently capable of eternal duration." Ashe also verified for himself the statements of the townsfolk that the mummies burned with great rapidity and noted that when he set a piece of a mummy aflame that it was "consumed with great violence."

In addition to the strange way in which the mummies burned, Ashe was also perplexed by the items he had collected and noted that even though he was quite well read, he had never heard of a tribe of North American Indians "who formed catacombs for their dead, or who were acquainted with the art of preservation by embalming." Ashe then went on to say, "The Egyptians, according to Herodotus, had three methods of embalming; but Diodorus observes that the ancient Egyptians had a fourth method, of far greater superiority. That manner is not mentioned by Diodorus. It has been extinct three thousand years, and yet I cannot think it presumptuous to conceive that the Indians were acquainted with it, or with a mode of equal virtue and effect." Ashe said this because, according to one of the townsfolk who saw the bodies, that the "...face and form and appearance of the whole body were so well preserved, that they must have been the exact representations of the living subject."

After examining the artifacts, Ashe placed them back in the tomb. He concluded,

I submit the fact for the consideration of a better judgement and an able pen and conclude by informing you that I restored every article to the catacomb; save some specimens retained as objects of the first curiosity, and blocking up the entry with the huge stones which originally closed it up, left the spot with the strongest emotions of veneration and displeasure: veneration for so sublime a monument of antiquity, and displeasure against the men whose barbarous and brutal hands reduced it to such a state of waste and desolation.

Despite Ashe's otherwise good credibility, many intellectuals and scholars seem to blindly dismiss Ashe's account of the Lexington Mummies. This may be because, to this day, the catacomb has never been rediscovered.

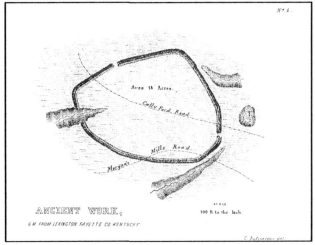

MOUNT HOREB EARTHWORK.

But who were these mysterious mummies? It is widely accepted that they lived in Kentucky long before the known Native American tribes of the area. Nor were the remains themselves that of indigenous peoples, so to speak, due to their having red hair and white skin, implying they might have been early-day explorers, perhaps even pre-dating Columbus.

However, modern academics shouldn't be so doubting of Ashe considering that years later some more puzzling archeological remains were found in Kentucky, completely undisputed this time. The best known are the Lexington Henge Gateway and the Mount Horeb earthworks.

It is thought that the Mount Horeb earthwork could be a ceremonial site leftover from the mysterious Adena culture, a strange tribe of Pre-Columbian Indians. This tribe was present in North America during the Early Woodland Period of 1,000 B.C. and possessed superior knowledge and weapons when compared to other peoples of the time. Their culture flourished for the next 800 years until it suddenly vanished. Is it possible then that they were the enigmatic inhabitants of the mummy catacomb found outside of Lexington?

Sources:

Ashe, Thomas. *Travels in America performed in 1806 : for the purpose of exploring the rivers Alleghany, Monongahela, Ohio, and Mississippi, and ascertaining the produce and condition of their banks and vicinity. Volume 1.* London, 1808.

Nunnelly, Barton M. *Mysterious Kentucky Vol. 2: The Dark and Bloody Ground.* 2017.

MUMMIES OF THE AMERICAS

In 1842, a Mormon publication, the *Times and Seasons* out of Nauvoo, Illinois, also printed a story on the mummies on May 2nd:

A CATACOMB OF
MUMMIES FOUND IN KENTUCKY

Lexington, in Kentucky, stands nearly on the site of an ancient town, which was of great extent and magnificence, as is amply evinced by the wide range of its circumvalliatory works, and the quantity of ground it once occupied. There was connected with the antiquities of this place, a catacomb, formed in the bowels of the limestone rock, about fifteen feet below the surface of the earth, adjacent to the town of Lexington. This grand object, so novel and extraordinary in this country, was discovered in 1775, by some of the first settlers, whose curiosity was excited by something remarkable in the character of the stones which covered the entrance to the cavern within. They removed these stones, and came to others of singular appearance for stones in a natural state; the removal of which laid open the mouth of a cave, deep, gloomy, and terrific, as they supposed.

With augmented numbers, and provided with light, they descended and entered, without obstruction, a spacious apartment; the sides and extreme ends were formed into niches and compartments, and occupied by figures representing men. When alarm subsided, and the sentiment of dismay and surprise permitted further research and inquiry, the figures were found to be mummies, preserved by the art of embalming, to as great a state of perfection as was known among the ancient Egyptians, eighteen hundred years before the Christian era; which was about the time that the Israelites were in bondage in Egypt, when this art was in its perfection.

The article then goes on to argue that these mummies were actually the descendants of the Israelites who came to America according to the Book of Mormon!

SATAN TEMPTING BOOTH TO THE MURDER OF THE PRESIDENT.

CHAPTER 5
CURSE OF THE ASSASSIN'S MUMMY

History tells us that on April 14, 1865, an actor named John Wilkes Booth assassinated Abraham Lincoln during a play at Ford's Theater.[5] And in that case, history would be correct. Where history becomes uncertain is upon Booth's death. According to accepted history, Booth fled on horseback towards Southern Maryland. Twelve days later, he was found within a barn on a farm in rural Northern Virginia. There he was shot through the neck and killed.

---

[5] Though General Robert E. Lee had surrendered and the Civil War was basically over, General Joseph E. Johnston was still fighting against the Union. In Booth's mind, the war wasn't over yet, and he and his other co-conspirators believed that killing Lincoln could aid the Confederacy.

FULL BODY VIEW OF THE BOOTH MUMMY.

However, much like Western outlaws Butch Cassidy, Billy the Kid, and Jesse James, there are stories that the wrong man was killed and Booth lived on. Theories abound as to why this happened, with some alleging that it was a government-endorsed conspiracy to fake Booth's death—either out of shame for not being able to apprehend him or because the government had, in fact, condoned the assassination. Whatever the case, Booth supposedly took on the alias of John St. Helen and moved to Texas, at first settling near Glen Rose before moving to Granbury, where he worked as a bartender.[6]

In 1877 in Granbury, St. Helen mistakenly believed that he was dying. On his "death bed," St. Helen confessed to a young lawyer he had worked with in the past, Finis L. Bates,[7] that he was, in fact, John Wilkes Booth. However, St. Helen pulled through and didn't die. Before fleeing Granbury, he explained to Bates that it was President Johnson himself who had authorized Lincoln's assassination. Johnson had even given Booth a special password allowing him to escape from authorities in on the plot. The man shot in the barn was just a random fugitive who was later passed off as Booth so that the real presidential assassin could slip away.

---

[6] Glen Rose and Granbury both are notable in the annals of Forteana and strange history. Glen Rose is the site of the hotly debated Paluxy River tracks where human footprints and dinosaur tracks were found imbedded in the limestone, creating quite a contradiction in the historical record. As for Granbury, it is the burial site of J. Frank Dalton, who claimed to be a surviving Jesse James! In 1976, Billy the Kid's long-missing tombstone was found in Granbury after having been stolen from Fort Sumner in 1950 shortly after a visit from Brushy Bill Roberts, a friend of Dalton's who likewise claimed to be Billy the Kid. Brushy Bill lived in Hico, Texas, not too far from Granbury. Clearly there is more to the story of Granbury being the home to presumed dead outlaws, though no one has been able to connect all the dots.
[7] Finis Bates met St. Helens when he represented him in an excise case. Bates is also famous actress Kathy Bates's grandfather.

VINTAGE POSTCARD OF GRANBURY.

Many years after his disappearance from Granbury, Booth/St. Helen resurfaced in the newspapers under the alias of David E. George. Bates just happened to read about the death of George, who committed suicide in Enid, Oklahoma, on January 13, 1903. What caught Bates's eye, naturally, was the detail that George claimed to be John Wilkes Booth!

According to the article, George had attempted suicide nine months earlier when he again thought he was dying. George confessed to the wife of a local Methodist preacher that "I am not David Elihu George. I am the one who killed the best man that ever lived. I am J. Wilkes Booth." Though the suicide attempt nine months earlier in 1902 had failed, George's second attempt did not. George had ingested a lethal amount of arsenic, which in turn also mummified his body.

DAVID E. GEORGE SHORTLY AFTER HIS
DEATH.

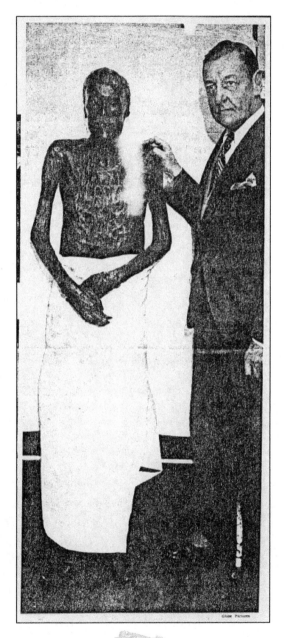

Globe Pictures

THE MUMMY ON DISPLAY.

Bates rushed to Enid upon reading the article in hopes of procuring Booth's mummified body. When he arrived, the body had further mummified thanks to the embalming fluid used by W.B. Penniman at his mortuary/furniture shop. However, Penniman himself wanted to use the unclaimed body as an attraction for his shop and refused to let Bates claim it. For several years, Booth's mummified corpse, now with glass eyes, sat upon the porch reading a newspaper. Bates found another way to exploit the wild story by writing a book, *Escape and Suicide of John Wilkes Booth: Written for the Correction of History,* in 1907. Around that same time, Bates did manage to finally procure the corpse itself. He did so with the help of an Oklahoma judge, who thought that Bates would actually bury the body since it was a former client of his. Instead, Bates rented out the notorious mummy to state fairs and carnivals. In his article on the mummy for History.com, Christopher Klein put it best when he wrote that the mummy "became a freak-show mirror image to the solemn funeral train procession taken by Lincoln's embalmed body in the weeks after the assassination."[8]

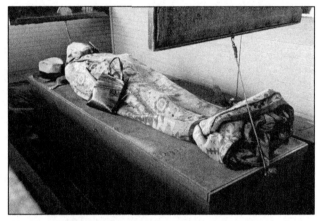

THE MUMMY UNDER WRAPS.

And like any good mummy, this one was cursed. The first inclination of the Booth Mummy's curse came when a circus train transporting the body crashed on its way to San Diego in 1920. Eight people died along with many of the so-called "freak show" animals on the train. Bates himself died not long after, and some like to claim it was due to the

---

[8] Klein, "The John Wilkes Booth Mummy That Toured America," History.com (April 17, 2015).
https://www.history.com/news/the-john-wilkes-booth-mummy-that-toured-america

ridicule he suffered from writing the book. The so-called Carnival King of the Southwest, William Evans, purchased the mummy from Bates's widow and began exhibiting it across the country as Bates had done. (Before purchasing it outright, Evans had merely been renting it from Bates.) The mummy eventually led to his financial ruin and Evans died when he was shot in a Chicago holdup in 1933.

As a *Saturday Evening Post* article published in 1938 put it, the mummy "scattered ill-luck around almost as freely as Tutankhamen is supposed to have done." The same article also stated that,

John [Wilkes Booth] has had a strange knockabout existence. He has been bought and sold, leased, held under bond, kidnapped and seized for debt; has been repeatedly chased out of town by local authorities for not having a license or for violating other ordinances; has been threatened with hanging by indignant G.A.R. veterans. Up until 1937 he has been a consistent money loser.[9]

You read that right. The Booth Mummy was at one point kidnapped and sentenced to be lynched before it was retrieved! When exactly this occurred is a bit murky. It is said it was stolen from Evans shortly after the train crash of 1920. *The Post* reported that,

---

[9] Johnston, "'JOHN WILKES BOOTH' ON TOUR,"
http://www.granburydepot.org/z/biog/BoothJohnWilkesOnTour.htm

Week after week Evans ran an advertisement in The Billboard, the Bible of the circus and carnival world, offering a reward of $1000 for information leading to the recovery of John. One day he met the alleged kidnaper on the street in San Diego. They had a knock-down-and-drag-out fight, ending in jail.[10]

There was another threat looming for the mummy. A court judge could, theoretically, insist upon the mummy's burial rather than its continued exploitation. As such, Evans really didn't want to take the kidnaper to court. Eventually, the mummy kidnapper came to Evans and told him, "I claim the reward. Pay me the $1000 and I'll return him in good condition." Incensed, but happy to have his mummy back, Evans agreed to pay $500 up front and the other $500 upon receiving the body. When he got the Booth Mummy back, he paid the kidnapper $500 via a rubber check (something akin to a hot check). So at least Evans only had to pay $500 rather than the full $1,000 for the kidnapped mummy.

The mummy received another new owner when it was purchased in 1932 for $5,000 by John Harkin. *The Post* article described Harkin as "the chief tattooed man of the Wallace-Hagenbeck circus." Having made a fortune in the circus and carnival business, Harkin invested his fortune in Chicago residential property and retired. It was likely in Chicago where he met Evans and bought

---

[10] Ibid.

the mummy off him in 1932. *The Post* reported that, "[The mummy] appealed strongly to Harkin because Harkin is a rugged individualist in his interpretation of history; he holds, for example, that Napoleon escaped after the Battle of Waterloo and that a dummy made up to resemble him was sent to St. Helena."[11]

Harkin and his wife exhibited the Booth Mummy across America in "a battered exhibition truck" which could be "converted into a small amusement palace." The Harkins apparently didn't fear the mummy, as it slept in between them on the floor of the truck (they slept in bunks on either side of it). The mummy wasn't always profitable, but it was particularly popular in Native American communities for some reason.

However, bad luck struck Harkin's real estate developments back in Chicago. It could be coincidence, of course, but most like to believe it was the mummy's curse.

Eventually, the Harkins became annexed, so to speak, by a bigger carnival operation owned by the Jay Gould Million-Dollar Show. *The Post* reported, "[Gould] is the first showman who had the genius to operate a modern American mummy successfully. After the million-dollar performance is completed, Gould steps to the loud-speaker, delivers a lecture on John, and crowds swarm to see him."[12]

---

[11] Ibid.
[12] Ibid.

Gould also remedied one of the biggest skeptical arguments against the mummy. No, not that it possibly wasn't John Wilkes Booth—that didn't seem to bother too many people—but that the mummy was real and not made of wax. *The Post* explained

Before Gould took general supervision over the attraction, its worst enemies were skeptics who would look at John and jeeringly exclaim

"Wax!" Mr. and Mrs. Harkin tremble with indignation at the mere mention of wax. Their $5000 historical and educational item has for years been up against the unfair competition of wax outlaws and heroes. Jay Gould solved this problem immediately. His first move on hitting a new town is to summon the undertakers, admit them free of charge and send them away raving. Even after decades of rough carnival and sideshow life, John is a masterpiece compared to the Pharaohs in the museums. He is as tough and leathery as a tackling dummy. One reason for this is that the Enid undertaker used arsenic in embalming the body. This is said to be the best preservative, but in recent years its use has generally been forbidden, because it may be employed to destroy the evidence in cases where murder has been perpetrated by arsenic. The fact that the suicide was by arsenic is said to have been an additional factor in preserving this mummy.[13]

The Booth Mummy continued touring the country well into the 1950s. Its history throughout the 1960s is sketchy—presumably it was mothballed for a time—and all we know is that the mummy was last seen sometime in the 1970s. Though the exact date of the last showing is never given in any sources, I did find reports that in 1977, an optometrist in Barberton, Ohio, claimed his family was in possession of the mummy. That same year,

---

[13] Ibid.

the *Sedalia Democrat* reported that the FBI was examining 18 missing pages recently found from Booth's old diary. Supposedly, these missing pages revealed much, such as that Booth claimed he was working for the secretary of war when he killed Lincoln. 1977 was a renaissance year for Booth as it even saw publication of another book detailing the theory that he survived into the 20th Century called *The Lincoln Conspiracy*. It was even made into a feature film.

Today the mummy is still missing, with reports stating that it's in the hands of a private collector somewhere. The Discovery Channel series *Mummies Unwrapped* did a segment on the missing Booth Mummy when they thought that they may have found the man who had it. The host, Ramy Romany, interviewed a man only identified as "Robert", a collector of human remains. However, to Romany's disappointment, it didn't turn out to be the Booth Mummy, but something else entirely called the "Pig-Tailed Man", which was born with a spinal deformity that gave the man a small "tail".

Much like the case of Billy the Kid and Brushy Bill Roberts, in later years there arose a cry for DNA testing on Booth's historically accepted body (i.e. not the mummy) and his brother. If the DNA matched, that would prove that Booth did indeed die back in 1865 just as the history books say. However, no DNA tests were ever conducted.

But, was the mummy really that of John Wilkes Booth? To attempt to answer that, we must return to the time when William Evans owned the mummy in the mid-to-late 1920s. At that time, Evans was approached by a Kansas City lawyer and Booth historian J.N. Wilkerson about the authenticity of the body. Wilkerson examined the mummy with Evans to look for distinctive physical traits that Booth had. For instance, Booth received a scar on his right eyebrow during a performance in *Richard III* when another actor slashed him over the right eye with the sword in the duel scene. To their shock, the mummy had the scar. Next, they sought out Booth's deformed right thumb, broken when a curtain fell on it. The mummy's right thumb was deformed. Lastly, they looked for a scar on the back of Booth's neck. It was there too.

Does this conclusively prove that the mummy and John Wilkes Booth were one and the same? Certainly not, but like his compatriots Billy the Kid and Jesse James, thanks to the mummy, the mystery of Booth's alleged in demise in 1865 still lingers to this day.

Sources:

Klein, Christopher. "The John Wilkes Booth Mummy That Toured America." History.com (April 17, 2015) https://www.history.com/news/the-john-wilkes-booth-mummy-that-toured-america

Johnston, Alva. "JOHN WILKES BOOTH' ON TOUR." *Saturday Evening Post* (February 10, 1938). http://www.granburydepot.org/z/biog/BoothJohnWilkesOnTour.htm

www.history.com/news/the-john-wilkes-booth-mummy-that-toured-america

ENTRANCE TO THE CAVE OF WINDS.

CHAPTER 6
MUMMY OF MANITOU CAVERNS

Located in Williams Canyon, a few miles northwest of Colorado Springs, you'll find the Cave of Winds, still one of the most popular tourist attractions in Colorado today.

According to local lore, the cave was used as a ceremonial spot for the Ute and Apache and might have served as an entrance to the underworld according to the Ute, while the Apache believed the cavern was home to a Great Spirit of the Wind. Supposedly, two schoolboys, John and George Pickett, found the entrance to the cave in 1880 and an exploration took place in June of that same year. The next year, the cave's first great promoter arrived: George Washington Snider.

**GEORGE SNIDER, LEFT, ALONG WITH
GEORGE AND JOHN PICKET AS ADULTS.**

Snider was a stonecutter from Ohio who found and explored a different section of the cave in 1881. He labeled his new discovery Canopy Hall due to its immense size. The room was about 200 feet long and housed thousands of stalactites and stalagmites. Snider saw the possibilities of a major tourist attraction and purchased the cave land from Frank Hemenway on January 29, 1881. Unfortunately for Snider, soon after making his discovery public, hordes of people descended into the cave to strip away many of the stalactites. Eventually, Snider's investment did pay off, and not only did he operate the Cave of Winds with a partner, but also a newly discovered cave he named Manitou Grand Caverns.

Tours were conducted by lantern at the time, and on some occasions Snider even held parties in the caverns.[14] Due to the darkness of the caves, Snider took delight in finding ways to frighten his customers. Actually, this is what led to the cavern's notoriety and success. When business began to lag, Snider got the idea to place a mummy within the cavern. His brother worked at a nearby quarry which just happened to unearth three mummies, which Snider speculated were probably the bodies of Utes. Though it took days of begging, Snider finally convinced his brother to sell him one of the mummies for a grand total of $5. Snider pretended/assumed that the mummy was that of a very important Ute, and would hide it within the cave. At just the right moment, he would surprise tourists with the mummy to get a good scare out of them.

The trick worked like a charm and Snider's business was booming. After a few months, Snider was well aware that word had gotten out as to whereabouts the mummy was hidden in the cave, thus lessening the surprise. Therefore, Snider

---

[14] To light the caverns, he paid young boys five cents an hour to stand around and hold lanterns. One day, after a party was held the previous night, the mother of some missing brothers came to see Snider to tell him that her boys never came home. Snider was both disturbed and perplexed. He had keys to the entrance, and had made sure to search the cavern thoroughly before locking up. Sadly, the two boys were never found in the cave or elsewhere.

endeavored to hide the mummy in a new spot as a way of surprising a group of college athletes that had booked a tour. Remarkably, when Snider went to move the mummy, it was gone!

CAVE OF WINDS ENTRANCE C. 1950s

As stated before, Snider was the only one who had access to the cavern and the entrance was sealed by a locked door—a door that only Snider had the key to. Plus, he had seen the mummy the day before it vanished. As such, one has to wonder just where the mummy went? It certainly didn't get up and walk out on its own...

As stated earlier, supposedly the Ute Native American tribe considered this cavern to be an entrance into the underworld. A legend even existed that a portal would open within the cave which allowed the spirits of the dead to pass to and fro. Perhaps the mummy fell into the portal and went to the underworld where it belonged?

Whatever happened to the mummy, be it mundane or supernatural, today the caverns are haunted. Tour guides have reported seeing people within the group tours that seemed to be dressed in the styles of the 19th Century. These same "people" were not present at the beginning of the tour and disappeared by the end of it. Spook lights have also been seen within the cave. One of the ghosts is even thought to be Snider himself, along with his wife.

Interestingly enough, on the night that Snider passed away in 1921, a severe lightning storm hit the valley. It produced a flood so intense that it caused a rockslide that sealed off the entrance to Snider's cave! The entrance remained sealed for 30 whole years. During the process of reopening and also after, the cave was plagued with bad luck—everything from odd lawsuits to freak accidents and even death. Odder yet, the cave was suddenly infested with grasshoppers and earthworms. In some cases, people disappeared into the caves never to be seen again. Due to the caves allegedly being the site of many Native American rituals, most people assume that the bad luck is attributed to that, and the mummy no doubt played a part as well.

CHAPTER 7
THE CONQUISTADOR MUMMY

California's Cantua Creek was named for José de Guadalupe Cantúa, a Spanish Army commander. Cantua and his troops were out on a mission to sequester the Native American population and bring them to the Mission San Juan when they discovered the creek sometime in the 19th Century. It would seem that due to the area's Spanish history when a mummy was found in the vicinity years later, it was speculated to be a conquistador—even though Cantua was certainly not old enough to be a conquistador. The *Evening World* out of New York reported on the story on December 16, 1890, on the front page:

A PETRIFIED GIANT.

He Is Seven Feet Long, Weighs 600 Pounds, and a Perfect Stranger.

[SPECIAL TO THE WORLD.]

FRESNO, CAL., Dec. 15.—The petrified body of a man has been brought here from Cantua Canyon, about sixty miles from town. The body was discovered by two men named Packwood and Barrett, who were building a dam. Part of the foot was exposed, and when the whole body was exhumed it was found to be wonderfully preserved. The body lay on a rock covered with earth, parts of it being buried to the depth of twelve feet. The body was straight and measured seven feet in length. The man was physically perfect. The face is clearly defined, the nose, eyes, forehead, mouth and chin being natural. The neck is long and rests on muscular shoulders. The arms are long and shapely, the left being folded high on the breast, with the hand resting near the throat, while the right comes diagonally across the body and rests on the stomach. The hair is gone, but the ears are clearly outlined. The hands are perfect, the nails and wrinkles in the skin of the fingers being as natural as life. The same may be said of the feet, the tendons showing the contraction familiar to physicians in cases of death from strychnine. The body weighs about six hundred pounds.

Cantua Canyon is dry most of the year. The indications are that the body had been buried for ages. In the same canyon is a petrified forest. The body is supposed to be of an early Spanish explorer. A glance at the petrification as well as the character of the discovers, preclude the idea of any deception like the "Solid Muldoon" giant fraud in Colorado. The curiosity will be sent to the California Academy of Sciences.

A PETRIFIED GIANT.
He Is Seven Feet Long, Weighs 600 Pounds, and a Perfect Stranger

[SPECIAL TO THE WORLD].

Fresno, Cal, Dec. I5.—The petrified body of a man has been brought here from Cantua Canyon, about sixty miles from town. The body was discovered by two men named Packwood and Barrett, who were building a dam. Part of the foot was exposed, and when the whole body was exhumed it was found to be wonderfully preserved. The body lay on a rock covered with earth, parts of it being buried to the depth of twelve feet. The body was straight and measured seven feet in length. The man was physically perfect. The face is clearly defined, the nose, eyes, forehead, mouth and chin having natural. The neck is long and rests on muscular shoulders. The arms are long and shapely, the left being folded high on the breast with the hand resting near the throat, while the right comes diagonally across the body and rests on the stomach. The hair is gone, but the ears are dearly outlined. The hands are perfect, the nails and wrinkles in the skin of the fingers being as natural as life. The same may be said of the feet, the tendons showing the contraction familiar to physicians in cases of death from strychnine. The body weighs about six hundred pounds. Cantua Canyon is dry most of the year. The indications are that the body had been buried for ages. In the same canyon is a petrified forest.

The body is supposed to be of an early Spanish explorer. A glance at the petrification as well as the character of the discovers, preclude the idea of any deception like the "Solid Muldoon" giant fraud in Colorado. The curiosity will be sent to the California Academy of Sciences.

CANTUA CREEK HISTORICAL MARKER.

A second, brief article on what may have been the same mummy—or, maybe not— appeared years later in the *Ukiah Republican Press* of July 1, 1892, which reported that,

FRESNO COUNTY.
The mummy which William Elkinton found in Cantua canyon and which the courts decided

that he must not keep because it was a human being and not property, has been stolen from the tomb where the health officer had sealed it up. Elkinton had been offered $2000 for it.

In an earlier article, the discoverers of the so-called "Spanish explorer" mummy were identified as Packwood and Barrett, not Elkinton. Was Elkinton a heretofore unmentioned partner of Packwood and Barrett? Or was this a different mummy discovered in the same spot? We'll likely never know. In any case, the first mummy was most likely not that of a conquistador at seven feet tall and 600 pounds! It does bring to mind the old horror film *Giant from the Unknown* (1958), which featured a giant conquistador zombie, though. The movie was also set in California. Coincidence?

The Omaha Daily Bee reported on another giant California mummy on October 10, 1891:

A Petrified Woman

Mr. I.N. Barret, a Council Bluffs gentleman who left the city last fall and spent the winter in Fresno, Cal., and signalized his stay there by the discovery of a petrified giant, which has attracted the attention of the scientific world, reached the city yesterday with another extraordinary petrification. He has rented the room, 537 Broadway, formerly occupied by Hart's jewelry store, and has placed the wonder on exhibition. It is a perfectly formed woman lying on her back with her hands peacefully folded across her breast. The corrugations of the skin on the hands can be traced to the minutest wrinkle, and every muscle is as natural as life. The face is classic, clean-cut and handsome, and the whole form conveys the impression that the woman, while peacefully sleeping in rosy health, was suddenly turned into stone. The drapery about the form has fallen away and petrified in little tufts, giving a ragged appearance in some places. The hair, eyelashes, finger and toe nails are clear and distinct, the former being petrified in tufts. A portion of the upper lip has been cut away revealing two teeth to which the enamel is still adhering. The petrification was found by a little boy within a few feet of where Barrett found the giant. It will be on exhibition here for two weeks.

CHAPTER 8
KING TUTS TOMB IN THE ARKANSAS VALLEY

Our story begins with the mysterious civilization known as the Mound Builders. To this day, no one knows who they were, though the most popular theory says that they were giants—Abraham Lincoln even mentioned them in a speech once—while others say they were a fairly advanced race of normal human beings. Whatever they were, their culture is thought to have spanned from roughly 3500 BCE to the 16th century CE.

These mounds extend across the Americas, but the ones we're going to discuss in this chapter are located in eastern Oklahoma. They were known collectively as the Spiro Mounds, but one in particular of special interest was alternatively known as both the Great Mortuary Mound and the

Craig Mound, after one of the landowners. They stretched about 300 feet long by 100 feet wide, their highest point measuring 33 feet at the peak. It could be a coincidence, but the number 33 has a great deal of occult significance. However, considering these same mounds also aligned to the sun during the equinox much like Stonehenge, it's probably no coincidence.

SPIRO MOUND C.1935 (DR. ROBERT E BELL)

People of the time believed that it was a burial ground for a long since vanished tribe of Native Americans. The mound was first sighted by a Choctaw named Rachel Brown, who used the nearby floodplain of the Arkansas River to grow crops. After a new barn was constructed near the mound to house mules, it didn't take long for Rachel to see that the mounds were haunted. The mules housed in the barn became so spooked and upset that they refused to work. Horses brought near the mound also became upset by something.

Indian Relics Unearthed In Oklahoma

Braden, Okla.—Indian relics—estimated to be from 600 to 2,000 years old and including the thigh bone of a giant brave—are being taken in large numbers from a huge burial mound 4 1-2 miles southwest of here.

The Pocola mining company, composed of six Arkansas and Oklahoma men, is in charge of excavations, begun last February.

Although it is a private enterprise, each item taken from the mound is catalogued and photographed, and careful records are being kept of the disposition of the artifacts, human bones, beads of wood and stone, pearls and large conch shells.

Situated in the middle of a field near the Arkansas river, the mound is approximately 100 feet long and 40 feet high at the peak. It is of sand, making digging comparatively easy. Excavations about 20 feet deep have been made.

Among the treasured finds is a large femur, indicating its owner must have been about nine feet tall. Bones and skeletons of other human beings are of normal size.

Charred remains, some with remnants of flesh still clinging to them, have been located, indicating the redskins of many centuries age

SPIRO MOUND C.1935 (DR. ROBERT E BELL)

While spooked animals were one thing, eventually Rachel bore witness to a strange sight that would seem right at home in one of the Ghostbusters films. In 1905, Rachel was startled from her sleep by a great noise. She went to the window to peer outside and saw a great blue flame shooting from the mound. Next, she saw what she described as a tiny wagon pulled by a team of cats emerging from the fire! The cat wagons then did circles in the air around the flames.[15] Over the years, others would also claim to see the phantom wagons—but no phantom cats that I know of—which were also out of proportion, either being in miniature form or sometimes appearing gigantic.

**EXCAVATIONS AT SPIRO MOUND C.1935
(DR. ROBERT E BELL)**

Eventually the property came under the ownership of William Craig, who remained protective of the mounds. In 1930, Craig passed away and his heirs decided to lease the site to pot hunters. Eventually was formed the Pocola Mining Company. For two years between 1933 and 1935, the site was mined of its priceless historical artifacts,

---

[15] Though the culture of the Spiro Mounds was more reminiscent of Mesoamerica than ancient Egypt, I think it's worth pointing out that cats were the guardians of the Egyptian underworld.

which included carved seashells, pearls, copper breastplates and other priceless items reminiscent of Mesoamerican culture. These items were sold to museums and private collectors alike.

**EXCAVATIONS AT SPIRO MOUND C.1935
(DR. ROBERT E BELL)**

One day in 1935, the excavators hit a petrified mud wall 26 feet down. In *Looting Spiro Mounds*, historian David La Vere wrote, "The pick blade broke through into empty space. Immediately there was a hissing noise, as humid Oklahoma summer air rushed into the hollow chamber beyond."[16] The main chamber had an eighteen-foot ceiling, and inside they found exceptionally well-preserved mummified bodies along with other well-preserved artifacts. The bodies, still dressed in colorful garments, were of little use to the simple-

---

[16] Robert, *It Happened in Oklahoma*, Kindle Edition.

minded pot hunters and were discarded.[17] Other than the mummies, the pot hunters took out every item they could get their hands on, though.

SPIRO MOUND PHOTOGRAPHED BY DR. ROBERT E BELL C.1935

Newspapers of the time touted the discovery as "American King Tut's Tomb." The discovery of King Tut's tomb was a sensationalized event when reported in 1922 and was still fresh in the American consciousness in 1935. The story of King Tut's tomb was further immortalized when members of the expedition that uncovered it began turning up dead, pointing to the now legendary curse of King Tut's tomb.

---

[17] Though not stated, it's possible that these mummies were giants. See the article on facing page opposite.

EXCAVATIONS AT SPIRO MOUND
(PHIL J. NEWKUMET)

And so too did a curse follow the discovery and ill-treatment of the mummies within the Great Mortuary Mound. The Pocola Mining Co. had lost several men during the excavation process, with one man being buried alive when a tunnel collapsed. While that could be chalked up to a typical mining accident, more suspicious were the deaths that occurred outside the mounds. Men were killed in car accidents and by strange illnesses, evoking shades of King Tut's Tomb. One of the lawyers representing the Pocola Mining Co. was mysteriously found dead alone in his office. The most chilling death of all was that of Reverend R.W. Wall, a local pastor who had aided Pocola Mining Co. in securing their lease. Wall was found drowned in a creek bed that had been dry for several weeks!

The curse apparently only extended to the careless miners of the Pocola Mining Co., though. A bit later, thanks to public outcry, the Oklahoma state legislature passed the Oklahoma Antiquities Law to protect archaeological sites and the Pocola Mining Co. got the boot. But not before dynamiting the great chamber before they left, sealing it off from a team of anthropologists from the University of Oklahoma. Humorously, they paid the curse no heed, and lead anthropologist Forrest Clements quipped, "The regular wages that come from this work—now that's something."

And indeed, no one from the anthropology department suffered the curse that we know of. Today the site is still being studied, and the ghosts seem to have been laid to rest since the days of Rachel Brown.

Sources:

Dorman, Robert. *It Happened in Oklahoma.* Globe Pequot, 2019.

CHAPTER 9
THE OUTLAW MUMMY

In life, Elmer McCurdy didn't amount to much, but in death was another story. In life, McCurdy was a second-class outlaw, perhaps born too late as he was too young to participate in the heyday of the Wild West. McCurdy was born in 1880 and began his inept reign of terror at the age of 31. I say inept because McCurdy's endeavors at bank and train robbery weren't terribly successful. Humorously, McCurdy had mishaps when he turned to using explosives during his crimes, often overestimating how much nitroglycerin was needed.[18]

For instance, in March of 1911, McCurdy and three outlaw companions successfully stopped a

---

[18] He had been trained to use nitroglycerin for demolition purposes during his time in the army.

train along the Iron Mountain-Missouri Pacific carrying $4,000. However, McCurdy rigged the safe with too much nitroglycerin and the safe, along with the money, was completely destroyed. Instead, McCurdy and his pals had to make due with the remains of silver coins which had melded into the safe's frame in the explosion. A similar incident occurred when McCurdy robbed a Kansas bank and destroyed the bank's interior.

McCurdy's last hurrah occurred that October in Okesa, Oklahoma. McCurdy and his compatriots set their sights on a train carrying $400,000, only they stopped the passenger car rather than the one containing the money. So instead they stole a measly $46 total from the mail clerk, some whiskey, and the conductor's watch. A newspaper later joked that it was "one of the smallest in the history of train robbery."

McCurdy sulked off to a friend's ranch to drink away his sorrows, and that's where he was captured. Early in the morning of October 7th, when McCurdy was still sleeping one off, three sheriffs tracked him down using bloodhounds and found him in a barn. In an interview in the October 8, 1911 edition of the *Daily Examiner*, Sheriff Bob Fenton said:

It began just about 7 o'clock. We were standing around waiting for him to come out when the first shot was fired at me. It missed me and he then turned his attention to my brother, Stringer Fenton. He shot three times at Stringer and when my brother got under cover he turned his attention to Dick Wallace. He kept shooting at all of us for about an hour. We fired back every time we could. We do not know who killed him ... (on the trail) we found one of the jugs of whiskey which was taken from the train. It was about empty. He was pretty drunk when he rode up to the ranch last night.

McCurdy's unremarkable career had come to an end. Similar to the case of David E. George (alias John Wilkes Booth), who died in Oklahoma a decade ago, McClurdy's body went unclaimed at the undertakers. Perhaps recalling the success of the Booth mummy, Joseph L. Johnson, the owner and undertaker, embalmed the body with an arsenic-based preservative. He then gave poor McCurdy a shave, dressed him in a suit, and stored him in the back of the funeral home. Then, taking another page from the Booth Mummy, Johnson decided to exploit him. However, Johnson was sly enough to realize that the McCurdy Mummy wasn't as big a deal as the Booth Mummy, who, after all, may have killed Abraham Lincoln. As such, Johnson humorously dressed his mummy in street clothes, placed a rifle in his hands, and called him "The Bandit Who Wouldn't Give Up" in reference to McCurdy's numerous failed robberies.[19] Johnson would then charge folks a whole nickel to come gawk at it.

---

[19] His other names included "The Mystery Man of Many Aliases", "The Oklahoma Outlaw", and "The Embalmed Bandit".

The mummy became so popular that it attracted offers from carnivals who wished to purchase it, but Johnson refused. Upon Johnson's refusal, the carnival owners got creative. In October of 1916, two men claiming to be McCurdy's brothers showed up and requested the body of their "brother" so they could give him a proper burial. Feeling it was the decent thing to do, Johnson allowed them to take the body back home. Only they didn't. One of the men was none other than James Patterson himself, of Great Patterson Carnival Shows (the other man was his brother Charles). The Patterson brothers then began exploiting Johnson's old mummy as "The Outlaw Who Would Never Be Captured Alive" in a traveling circus. This lasted until 1922 when Patterson sold his circus to Louis Sonney.

Appropriately, Sonney featured the McCurdy Mummy in his traveling Museum of Crime, which also included wax replicas of Bill Doolin and Jesse James. By 1928, McCurdy changed hands again to be a part of the official sideshow of the Trans-American Footrace. Then, in 1933, McCurdy was exploited by a man named Dwain Esper to promote his exploitation film *Narcotic*. Poor McCurdy was himself now playing a part as the body of a "dead dope fiend" on display in the theater lobby. Esper claimed that the dead man had been gunned down after robbing a drug store to support his habit. As it turned out, this was McCurdy's start in the acting business. It was also at this point that he was less of an embalmed corpse and more of a mummy, as his skin had hardened a great deal and the body began to shrivel. (Esper claimed that the skin's appearance was due to his drug use!)

LOUIS SONNEY AND HIS TRAVELING SHOW.

The mummy was put in storage in a Los Angeles warehouse and resurfaced again in 1964, when it was lent to filmmaker David F. Friedman for his movie, *She Freak*, released in 1967. The next year, the body was part of a $10,000 sale along with some wax figures to the Hollywood Wax Museum. McCurdy then got a gig at a show at Mount Rushmore; only he was damaged during a windstorm that blew off the tips of his ears, fingers, and toes. Poor McCurdy was then dropped for looking "too gruesome" and not looking lifelike enough to exhibit. No longer in the bigtime, poor McCurdy was sold off to The Pike, an amusement park in Long Beach, California. He worked there until 1976, but like some of the more fortunate actors, McCurdy was destined for a comeback.

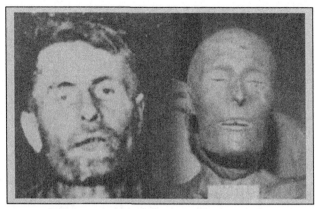

MCCURDY SHORTLY AFTER DEATH AND AS A MUMMY.

McCurdy's big break came from sheer luck, as it turned out. In December of 1976, the crew of *The Six Million Dollar Man* TV series was filming scenes for their "Carnival of Spies" episode at The Pike. McCurdy was just hanging around set, literally from a makeshift gallows, when one of the crew thought he was just a nobody and decided to move him out of the way. To his shock, the arm of what he assumed to be a plastic dummy broke right off, exposing bone and dried out muscle tissue. Seeing as how they had a real body on their hands, the crew called the police. An autopsy was performed, and of all things, a ticket stub found in the mouth helped the authorities uncover the mummy's identity. The stub was for Louis Sonney's Museum of Crime, and so the police contacted Sonney's son, Dan, who was able to confirm that the body was that of McCurdy.

ELMER McCURDY
ALLIAS FRANK CURTIS
FRANK DAVIDSON
SHOT BY SHERIFF POSE
NEAR PAWHUSKA.OKLA
10-7-1911

Though McCurdy didn't get to appear on *The Six Million Dollar Man,* he got something much better: a proper burial. McCurdy made headlines more significantly than he ever had before, and funeral homes were now offering to bury him for free. Ultimately, he was shipped back to Oklahoma under the care of the Indian Territory Posse of

Oklahoma Westerns. On April 22, 1977, a funeral procession took McCurdy to the Boot Hill section of the Summit View Cemetery in Guthrie, Oklahoma. Three hundred people attended his graveside service, and appropriately, he was buried next to his old pal Bill Doolin. The two didn't know each other in life, but McCurdy had toured with Doolin's wax mannequin on the road. Knowing how people could be with old outlaws, two feet of concrete were poured over his casket, an honor usually afforded to sensational outlaws like Billy the Kid. So, as it turned out, in his own strange way, McCurdy had finally made the "big time."

CHAPTER 10
MUMMIES OF MAMMOTH CAVE

Believe it or not, the world's longest cave system can be found stretching across three counties (Edmonson, Glasgow and Warren) within Kentucky. At over six hundred miles long, Kentucky's Mammoth Cave is aptly named. It was discovered in the late 1790s by Francis Houchin when he was out bear-hunting. He had just shot and wounded a bear, which took refuge in a cave in the vicinity of Green River. In 1897, it was formally mapped out by Valentine Simons, and by 1812 it was purchased by Charles Wilkins and Hyman Gratz. The huge caverns were subsequently mined for calcium nitrate on an industrial scale via slave labor. Eventually the men in the mines would come across several mummified remains as well.

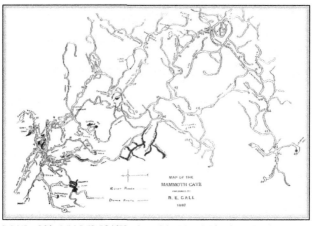

MAP OF MAMMOTH CAVE BY R.E. CALL C. 1897

The first mummy was discovered a year previous to the purchase by Wilkins and Gratz in 1811. The mummy was small and was appropriately found in "Short Cave," four miles south of Mammoth Cave in Barren County. However, when miners exposed this baby mummy to sunlight, all but the skull crumbled to dust due to the elements.

When Wilkins later found out about the mummies, he realized that he could start exploiting them to onlookers for a fee. In the hopes of discovering more mummies, he offered a reward to anyone who found them. (This was also done because if there was no reward, any mummies might simply be burned in a fire heap to get them out of the way.) Two years later, Wilkins got his wish and another body was found in Short Cave. Miners were digging into the clay floor when their shovels struck a solid mass. It turned out to be a four-foot by four-foot limestone slab, which, when removed, unveiled itself to be the lid of a crypt belonging to another mummy, this one an adult female. It was in a sitting positing with the knees drawn up towards the head, hands resting on the knees. Although this wouldn't be learned until sixty years later, it turned out the woman was more carefully embalmed than even the ancient Egyptians had done. That wasn't the only way in which the corpse differed from what was presumed to be a Native American. It was unusually tall for a woman at six feet and had close-cropped red hair.

The mummy was given the name of "Fawn Hoof" and promptly displayed at Mammoth Cave right away. In 1814, two more mummies were found again in Short Cave. Like Fawn Hoof, they too were found in a sitting position and had red hair. Almost immediately after their discovery, one mummy was acquired by John Scudder, who put it on display in his museum in New York City, while the other was shipped off to the Cincinnati Museum in Cincinnati, Ohio. Though records of the height of the two mummies have never surfaced, there does at least exist an astute observation of the New York mummy made by Dr. Samuel L. Mitchill, editor of a New York scientific and medical journal. In a letter to a friend published on August 24, 1815, Mitchill wrote:

Dear Sir: I offer you some observations on a curious piece of American antiquity now in New York. It is a human body: found in one of the limestone caverns of Kentucky. It is a perfect desiccation; all the fluids are dried up. The skin, bones, and other firm parts are in a state of entire preservation. I think it enough to have puzzled Bryant and all the archaeologists. This was found in exploring a calcareous cave in the neighborhood of Glasgow for saltpeter. These recesses, though underground, are yet dry enough to attract and retain the nitric acid. It combines with lime and potash; and probably the earthy matter of these excavations contains a good proportion of calcareous carbonate. Amidst them drying and antiseptic ingredients, it may be conceived that putrefaction would be stayed, and the solids preserved from decay. The outer envelope of the body is a deer-skin, probably dried in the usual way, and perhaps softened before its application by rubbing. The next covering is a deer's skin, whose hair had been cut away by a sharp instrument resembling a batter's knife. The remnant of the hair and the gashes in the skin nearly resemble a sheared pelt of beaver. The next wrapper is of cloth made of twine doubled and twisted. But the thread does not appear to have been formed by the wheel, nor the web by the loom. The warp and filling seem to have been crossed and knotted by an operation like that of the fabric of the northwest coast, and of the Sandwich Islands. Such a botanist as the lamented Muhlenbergh could determine the plant which furnished the fibrous material.

The innermost tegument is a mantle of cloth, like the preceding, but furnished with large brown feathers, arranged and fashioned with great art, so as to be capable of guarding the living wearer from wet and cold. The plumage is distinct and entire, and the whole bears a near similitude to the feathery cloaks now worn by the nations of the northwestern coast of America. A. Wilson might tell from what bird they were derived.

The body is in a squatting posture, with the right arm reclining forward, and its hand encircling the right leg. The left arm hangs down, with its hand inclined partly under the seat. The individual, who was a male, did not probably exceed the age of fourteen at his death. There is near the occiput a deep and extensive fracture of the skull, which probably killed him. The skin has sustained little injury; it is of a dusky color, but the natural hue cannot be decided with exactness, from its present appearance. The scalp, with small exceptions, is covered with sorrel or foxy hair. The teeth are white and sound. The hands and feet, in their shriveled state, are slender and delicate. All this is worthy the investigation of our acute and perspicacious colleague, Dr. Holmes. There is nothing bituminous or aromatic in or about the body, like the Egyptian mummies, nor are there bandages around any part. Except the several wrappers, the body is totally naked. There is no sign of a suture or incision about the belly; whence it seems that the viscera were not removed. It may now be expected that I should offer some opinion as to the antiquity and race of this singular execution. First, then, I am satisfied that it does not belong to that class of white men of which we are members. Secondly; nor do I believe that it ought to be referred to the bands of Spanish adventurers, who, between the years 1500 and 1600, rambled up the Mississippi, and along its tributary streams. But on this head I should like to know the opinion of my learned and sagacious friend, Noah Webster. Thirdly; I am equally obliged to reject the opinion that it belonged to any of the tribes of aborigines, now or lately inhabiting Kentucky. Fourthly; the mantle of the feathered work, and the mantle of twisted threads, so nearly resemble the fabric of the indigenous of Wakash and the Pacific Islands, that I refer this individual to that era of time, and that generation of men, which preceded the Indians of the Green River, and of the place where these relics were found. This conclusion is strengthened by the consideration that such manufactures are not prepared by the actual and resident red men of the present day. If the Abbe Clavigero had had this case before him, he would have thought of the people who constructed those ancient forts and mounds, whose exact history no man living can give. But I forbear to enlarge; my intention being merely to manifest my respect to the society for having enrolled me among its members, and to invite the attention of its Antiquarians to further inquiry on a subject of such curiosity.

With respect, I remain yours,
-Samuel L. Mitchill.

After Scudder's passing in 1841, P. T. Barnum bought the museum and rechristened it Barnum's American Museum. Unfortunately, it burned to the ground in 1865 and the mummy along with it. And this is where the story starts to get weird. Remember the other mummy found around the same time, the one that got shipped off to Cincinnati? Well, that museum burned down, too, as it turned out. (Not the same year; that fire didn't occur until 1944.) Were the two mummies cursed? Or was someone trying to cover up their existence?

MAMMOTH CAVE'S OTHER MUMMIES

There are two other mummies that "survived" their exploitation after being discovered in Mammoth Cave, though. However, both were children, so their stature wasn't really eyebrow raising when compared to Fawn Hoof. The first was Little Alice, who actually turned out to be Little Al, discovered in 1865. This small body was later found to be a male child though at first it was mistaken for a female. It was found in Salt Cave rather than Short Cave, and was displayed in Mammoth Cave all the way into the 1950s. Alongside her was Lost John, the last of the mummies, found in 1935. The little five-year-old had been mining gypsum in the cave when a six ton rock collapsed upon him. However, unlike the original four mummies, Lost John did appear to be Native American, as no one ever described red hair on him.

Though she didn't perish in flames, Fawn Hoof would also disappear from public record. Until 1915, she attracted thousands of spectators to gaze upon the so-called "Indian Princess." Fawn Hoof attained international attention upon her 1915 purchase by Nahum Ward, who took her on tour. His fictional account of how he had discovered her himself in Mammoth Cave became a success both in the States and also in London.

Fawn Hoof changed hands again in 1917 when she was sold to the American Antiquarian Society of Worcester, Massachusetts. Unfortunately, by this point, the years on tour had taken their toll, and over time spectators had managed to pluck various pieces off of the mummy, including an entire arm, some teeth, and pieces of hair. Today, Fawn Hoof's remains have conveniently vanished, and some whisper it's due to her heritage as a female giant...

CHAPTER II
THE MARTIAN MUMMY

One of the strangest mummies of the Americas may well rest in a lonely Texas cemetery in the tiny settlement of Aurora. That's because the body in question might belong to a Martian. I am speaking, of course, of the famous Aurora, Texas UFO crash of 1897 wherein an alien was supposedly buried in the cemetery. As odd as that story may sound, the United States was in the midst of a massive airship flap that year, and hundreds of stories appeared detailing sightings of futuristic dirigibles in the clouds. The stranger tales told of alien occupants, and Aurora's story was the strangest of them all.

ARTIST'S RENDITION OF CRASH BY NEIL RIEBE.

On April 17, 1897, at 6 o'clock in the morning, a silver-colored, cigar-shaped UFO soared across the skies. The newspaper account detailing the story by Aurora resident S. E. Haydon that appeared in the *Dallas Morning News* stated that:

A Windmill Demolishes It

Aurora, Wise Co., Tex., April 17.—(To The News.)—About 6 o'clock this morning the early risers of Aurora were astonished at the sudden appearance of the airship which has been sailing through the country.

It was traveling due north, and much nearer the earth than ever before. Evidently some of the machinery was out of order, for it was making a speed of only ten or twelve miles an hour and gradually settling toward the earth. It sailed directly over the public square, and when it reached the north part of town collided with the tower of Judge Proctor's windmill and went to pieces with a terrific explosion, scattering debris over several acres of ground, wrecking the windmill and water tank and destroying the judge's dower garden.

The pilot of the ship is supposed to have been the only one on board, and while his remains are badly disfigured, enough or the original has been picked up to show that he was not an inhabitant of this world. Mr. T. J. Weems, the United States signal service officer at this place and an authority on astronomy, gives it as his opinion that he was a native of the planet Mars.

Papers found on his person—evidently the record of his travels—are written in some unknown hieroglyphics, and can not be deciphered.

The ship was too badly wrecked to form any conclusion as to Us construction or motive power. It was built of an unknown metal, resembling somewhat a mixture of aluminum and silver, and it must have weighed several tons.

The town is full of people to-day who are viewing the wreck and gathering specimens of the strange metal from the debris. The pilot's funeral will take place at noon to-morrow.

S.E. HAYDON.

A Windmill Demolishes It.

Aurora, Wise Co., Tex., April 17.—(To The News.)—About 6 o'clock this morning the early risers of Aurora were astonished at the sudden appearance of the airship which has been sailing through the country.

It was traveling due north, and much nearer the earth than ever before. Evidently some of the machinery was out of order, for it was making a speed of only ten or twelve miles an hour and gradually settling toward the earth. It sailed directly over the public square, and when it reached the north part of town collided with the tower of Judge Proctor's windmill and went to pieces with a terrific explosion, scattering debris over several acres of ground, wrecking the windmill and water tank and destroying the judge's flower garden.

The pilot of the ship is supposed to have been the only one on board, and while his remains are badly disfigured, enough of the original has been picked up to show that he was not an inhabitant of this world.

Mr. T. J. Weems, the United States signal service officer at this place and an authority on astronomy, gives it as his opinion that he was a native of the planet Mars.

Papers found on his person—evidently the record of his travels—are written in some unknown hieroglyphics, and can not be deciphered.

The ship was too badly wrecked to form any conclusion as to its construction or motive power. It was built of an unknown metal, resembling somewhat a mixture of aluminum and silver, and it must have weighed several tons.

The town is full of people to-day who are viewing the wreck and gathering specimens of the strange metal from the debris. The pilot's funeral will take place at noon to-morrow.

S. E. HAYDON.

ACTUAL ARTICLE FROM DALLAS
MORNING NEWS, 4-19-1897

To this day it's hotly debated as to whether the story was a simple case of yellow journalism or quite possibly one of the first major recorded UFO crashes. Hoax or not, the tale is recounted on an official Texas State Historical Marker, which is rare for UFO cases.

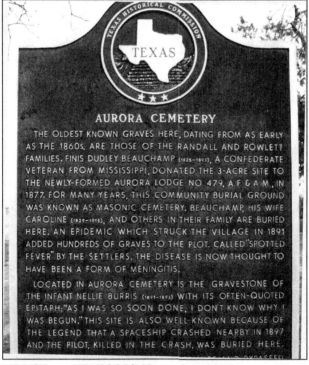

STATE HISTORICAL MARKER AT AURORA CEMETERY (PHOTO BY NOE TORRES)

When the pilot was buried, a special grave marker was erected at the site. In 1973, newspaper reporter Bill Case, who was also the state director for Texas MUFON, described the marker as having a drawing on it of a flying saucer with portholes. Case used a metal detector over the spot and became excited when it indicated that large pieces of metal were also buried there—possibly alien wreckage. When he asked permission to exhume the grave he was unfortunately denied. Worse still, shortly after Case wrote the story, thieves stole the marker. Over time, the exact location of the pilot's body became unclear due to several of the grave markers going missing. Today, nobody is exactly sure where the pilot was buried.

ARTIST NEIL RIEBE'S SKETCH OF THE ORIGINAL GRAVE OF THE AURORA SPACEMAN.

In 2008, an unmarked grave dating to the 1890s was found at the Aurora Cemetery during the filming of a television show called "UFO Hunters" for the History Channel. Since the owners of the cemetery will not allow anyone to dig up the grave, nobody knows if it is the grave of the strange pilot or not.

GUANAJUATO MUMMIES C.1940s.

CHAPTER 12
MEXICO'S MUMMIES

One of the most famous mummy exhibits in the world is located not in Egypt, but in Mexico; that place being The Mummies' Museum in Guanajuato, Mexico.

The mummified remains were the result of an 1833 cholera outbreak and the resulting cemetery created in its wake. Many years later, a local tax was instigated which necessitated that all perpetual burials had to pay a fee! Relatives of the dead who could not be located, or those who could not pay, had their dead disinterred! This occurred sometime between the 1870s and the 1950s as far as most can tell.

To everyone's shock, the bodies were incredibly well preserved. It is thought this happened in part due to Guanajuato's natural climate coupled with many of the bodies having been embalmed. Cemetery workers stored the better-preserved bodies in a building and began charging curious onlookers a few pesos each to view them! By 1969, the mummies had become so popular that the El Museo de las Momias ("The Museum of the Mummies") was born and today houses a rotating display of about 111 mummies.

**VINTAGE POSTCARD
WITH GUANAJUATO MUMMIES AS
PHOTOGRAPHED IN EARLY 1900s.**

The mummies aren't just unique for their exceptional preservation; many of them have expressions of terror etched into their faces. Most of these occurred naturally in post-mortem, but at least one woman was buried alive by accident. Ignacia Aguilar suffered from a rare condition that made it appear as if her heart had stopped beating. During one of these times, when her heart appeared to have stopped beating for an entire day, she was buried. Later, when she was disinterred, it was clear that her mummy was biting its own arm in agony.

GUANAJUATO, MEXICO.

Robert Bitto of Mexico Unexplained managed to find at least one urban legend where of one of the mummies came to life. According to the story, a man visiting Guanajuato for a business conference went to visit the museum. It was a slow day there and as the ticket taker made small talk with the visitor, he informed him that he had come at an opportune time—not just because the museum wasn't crowded, but because 36 mummies had just returned to the museum after touring the United States for four years. For the first time in years, the museum's collection was complete. Or so it would seem.

As the man walked among the mummies, he noticed a spot where a body appeared to be missing. After all, the spot was conspicuously empty, so a mummy must have occupied that space at one point. The man left the museum to walk to his hotel, which was nearby. Suddenly, he witnessed a car hit a woman on the street. He ran towards the accident and could see that the woman appeared to be wearing very old clothing, and a silk scarf obscured her face from view. As the man came upon the old woman, she grabbed his hand and chills ran up his spine. Her hand looked just like one of the mummies.

The man apparently never saw her face but heard her speak when she said to him, "Welcome to Guanajuato. And thank you."[20] The man closed his eyes and shook his head in disbelief. When he opened his eyes, the mummy was gone. This is

---

[20] https://mexicounexplained.com/5-brief-legends-guanajuato

most likely a made-up ghost story to benefit the museum, but it was worth including, obviously.

POSTER FOR "THE MUMMIES OF GUANAJUATO" WHERE LUCHADOR SANTOS FIGHTS THE MUMMIES!

The mummies had a profound effect on sci-fi author Ray Bradbury when he toured the museum. The chilling visit swiftly resulted in a story from

Bradbury entitled "The Next in Line." In his introduction to *The Stories of Ray Bradbury*, the author recollected:

> The experience so wounded and terrified me, I could hardly wait to flee Mexico. I had nightmares about dying and having to remain in the halls of the dead with those propped and wired bodies. In order to purge my terror, instantly, I wrote 'The Next in Line.' One of the few times that an experience yielded results almost on the spot.

The mummies have a few other claims to horror fame. Notably, they were utilized in the opening credits of Werner Herzog's remake of *Nosferatu the Vampyre* (1979). Then there is *Santo vs. The Mummies of Guanajuato* (1970), which had the Mexican wrestler/superhero Santo battle reanimated mummies from the museum. Ed Wood, the notorious filmmaker responsible for *Plan 9 from Outer Space*, planned a whole movie to revolve around the mummies called *The Day the Mummies Danced* in the mid-1970s as well, though it never happened.

Sources:

Bitto, Robert. "5 Brief Legends of Guanajuato." Mexico Unexplained. https://mexicounexplained.com/5-brief-legends-guanajuato

The Mummy of Majalca

What's about to follow is really nothing more than a modern ghost story, but it's still too good to pass up. (Nor does it necessarily fit this book's time period of the late 19th and early 20th Century.) At an undisclosed time years ago, five people went on a camping trip to Cumbres de Majalca National Park, 55 miles northeast of Chihuahua City, Mexico. One of the young men's mothers had cautioned them about a local legend involving a magical mummy within Majalca, which they naturally ignored.

Outside of the park, their vehicle suffered a flat tire and they were forced to pull over to change it. One of the men, named Luis, wandered away to be alone and sat among a small outcrop of rocks. Suddenly a glint between the stones caught his eye. He began tossing the rocks aside and called to his friends. Eventually, he unearthed a mysterious black box five feet long. As it turned out, it wasn't just a box. It was a coffin. As he pried the lid off, he saw the form of a bejeweled mummy within it. Notably, there was a gold ring on its right hand. Most of the group were too superstitious to take any of the riches for fear of a curse, except for Luis, who plucked off the ring.

However, in doing so, he tore off the entire right hand of the mummy. A greenish-red liquid spurted out of the severed arm and onto Luis, who soon found it hard to breathe. He was also becoming very pale. Apparently, their flat tire had yet to be fixed, and nor could Luis wait. They frantically began scanning the lonely road for a car. Miraculously, one appeared. But it was a small car driven by an old woman, and there was room for only one passenger. The injured Luis hopped inside as the woman told him she could take him to a hospital in Chihuahua City.

As the car sped away, Luis suddenly took note of the fact that the woman was missing her right hand. Startled, Luis asked what had happened to it. She replied that he had taken it from her. She was the ghost of the mummy! (Somehow driving a car!) Later, Luis's friends found his dead body along Highway 45. The cause of death was ruled as a heart attack.

CHAPTER 13
THE CARDIFF GIANT

You've heard the old adage not to take any wooden nickels, but what about wooden mummies? On October 16, 1869, when two diggers were sinking a well on the property of William Newell in Cardiff, New York, something truly incredible was unearthed. "I declare, some old Indian has been buried here!" one of the diggers exclaimed upon striking the solid form of a man in the earth. But it wasn't just any man, it was a giant. And it wasn't just any giant, either, it was a petrified giant!

The body measured ten feet and quickly became a sensation as onlookers swarmed the farm to get a look. On the first day, no fees were charged. By the second day, a tent had been set up and visitors were to pay fifty cents for a fifteen minute visit with the giant. Soon, people were swarming the farm in the hundreds and Newell was making a killing off of the body. The town itself was also quite happy, as money was also pumped into the local economy at hotels and local eateries.

EXHUMATION OF THE CARDIFF GIANT.

Doubt was cast upon the discovery early on, as some rightly assumed it was really a wooden statue, not a petrified man. John F. Boynton, a geologist, theorized that the statue was carved by a French Jesuit in the 16th or 17th century. Andrew D. White, the first president of Cornell University, made no gestures to explain the giant as anything other than a hoax.

Of course, he was right. The Cardiff Giant, as it was by then called, was really the product of a New York tobacconist named George Hull. Though the

money he could make from perpetrating such a hoax surely crossed his mind, his motivation was initially politically driven. Hull was one of the early atheist evolutionists and had recently gotten into an argument with a preacher about the existence of the Biblical giants. Hull then decided he would create a fake giant to show how quickly the masses could be fooled, and maybe make a few bucks along the way...

In Fort Dodge, Iowa, in 1868, Hull and an accomplice, H.B. Martin, hired men to exhume a ten-foot block of gypsum under the auspices that it would be used as a monument to Abraham Lincoln in New York. The huge granite block was shipped to Edward Burghardt, a German stonecutter in Chicago, who would then create the Cardiff Giant in secrecy. In turn, Burghardt hired two sculptors, Henry Salle and Fred Mohrmann, to help him mold the faux giant. To ensure that it looked as though it had been buried for many years, an assortment of acids and stains were used to age it. In addition to this, the body was poked with sturdy, steel knitting needles to make pores. All in all, the endeavor cost Hull $2,600.

By November of 1868, Hull's creation was finished and he transported it by train to his cousin's farm. A patient man, he waited nearly an entire year to instruct his cousin to call on the diggers to come work on the well.

As Hull raked in the money, a New York syndicate took notice and bought the Cardiff Giant for $23,000. In turn, the famous showman P. T. Barnum offered the syndicate $50,000 for the giant. They refused, and so Barnum had his own fake made of the fake! Eventually this all led to a lawsuit which in turn cast a more scrutinous eye upon both giants. By December of that same year, Hull admitted that both were fakes. This ironically saved Barnum from a lawsuit himself since he had created a fake off of another fake! Or, in other words, Barnum couldn't be sued for the false advertising of a real giant since the original Cardiff Giant was itself a fake.

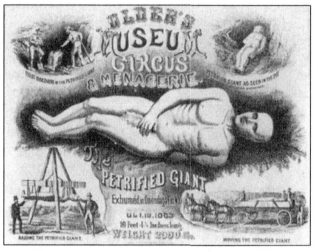

After this, the Cardiff Giant naturally began its descent into obscurity. Though it still appeared in traveling shows as a novelty/curiosity, the jig was up. The wooden carcass was procured by the Farmers' Museum in Cooperstown, New York, in 1947 and resides there to this day.

Though it makes for an interesting story, the worst thing about the Cardiff Giant is that it hurt the credibility of other giant mummy finds, which are actually quite numerous...

THE SOLID MULDOON

The Cardiff Giant story has a sequel in the form of the Solid Muldoon. Of course, there were several notable petrified human hoaxes over the years, but this one is notable because it, too, was the product of George Hull.

Eight years after the Cardiff Giant fiasco, in 1877, another petrified man was unearthed at Mace's Hole, near Beulah, Colorado. Because the body was hard as a rock, it was called the Solid Muldoon after a popular wrestler of the time, William Muldoon, who was nicknamed "The Solid Man".

Rather than being carved out of granite, the Solid Muldoon was a mixture of mortar, rock dust, clay, and plaster with some ground bones, blood and meat thrown in for good measure, making it something of a modern day Gollum. Hull had it kiln-fired over the course of several days before burying it near Mace's Hole.

As opposed to a whole year, this time he only waited three months to have it "discovered". One day a local fossil hunter named William Conant was eating his lunch in the area when he spotted an unusual rock that seemed to resemble a human foot. As he began to investigate the odd formation, he learned it was the bottom part of a seven-foot tall body buried in the earth. Using a pick-ax to remove the body from the roots of a cedar tree it was entangled within, he eventually unearthed it and took it to Pueblo, Colorado, where it was swiftly put on display.

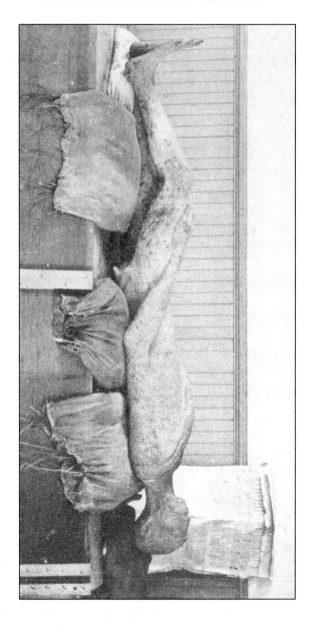

It didn't take long for experts to denounce this second petrified man as an ancient sculpture—again missing the fact that it was another modern hoax. History continued to repeat itself as the figure was successfully exhibited, attracting the attention of P.T. Barnum again.

However, whereas last time Hull's hoax was a jab at the giants of Christianity, this time Hull was either making fun of or trying to bolster the theory of evolution. The arms were long and ape-like, and the backbone protruded as though it had once been a tail!

Eventually it was revealed that Hull had struck again, and the second petrified man was forgotten even more quickly than the first.

CHAPTER 14
DEATH VALLEYS CITY OF THE DEAD

eath Valley is renowned the world over as being one of the hottest, driest, and most desolate places on the planet. It was aptly named by the 49ers during the California Gold Rush in the mid-1800s. However, according to the legend of the Shoshone tribe, Death Valley was once a beautiful, lush valley teaming with life.

According to myth, the area was ruled over by a beautiful, unnamed queen. Her beauty was only skin-deep, though. She was vain and desired a huge temple that would make the ones of the Aztecs to the south pale by comparison. She ordered her people to begin construction on her palace and had them transport stone, quartz, marble, and timber from faraway lands to begin the process. The people worked arduously to complete the task at hand, but the process took longer than the Queen desired, and she feared she would be an old crone by the time it was completed. In a short span, she transitioned from a beloved queen to a despised dictator. She turned her tribe into slaves, lashing their backs with the whip to quicken their pace. Once, she even whipped her own daughter for working too slowly. In her state of exhaustion, the lashing was too much for the girl who began to expire. In her dying breaths, she cursed her mother and her kingdom. It was then that Death Valley became what it is today. The sun increased its heat. The streams and lakes evaporated, plants withered and died, and the animals ran away. Today it is said that the Queen's half-finished palace can be glimpsed in the distance as a mirage.

According to another myth, Death Valley is home to the legendary Paiute Kingdom of Shin-au-av (alternately meaning "God's Land" or "Ghost Land"). Thousands of years ago, an unnamed Paiute chief suffered the death of his wife. Like one of the Greek heroes of old, he decided to descend into the underworld to rescue her. In this case, he literally entered a cave in Death Valley that led him through various tunnels and underground passages where he had to battle various demons and monsters. Eventually, he could literally see the light at the end of the tunnel across a very narrow rock bridge spanning a bottomless chasm à la *Indiana Jones and the Last Crusade.* It was this chasm that truly separated the land of the living from the land of the dead.

ANSEL ADAMS DEATH VALLEY.

He crossed the bridge and soon reached a new land comprised of lush, green meadows. It was ruled over by the daughter of Chief Shin-au-av, a beautiful virgin so impressed by this chief from the surface world that she offered herself to him. She became even more impressed when he declined her advances to keep searching for his wife. Rather than being spiteful, she took the chief's hand and led him to a huge, natural amphitheater where he could see thousands of deceased Paiute enjoying the afterlife and dancing in a circle. The chief asked Princess Shin-au-av how he could find his wife in the huge mass of swirling dancers. She advised him to sit and wait, then to grab his wife when she passed by. Then, he could return with her to the surface. But, as with all fairytales, there was a caveat. Once he took her hand, he could never look back.

DEATH VALLEY BOOKLET.

After three days of waiting, the chief finally spotted his wife from the huge procession and grabbed her to return to the surface. Much like Lot's wife, the chief's wife couldn't resist one last look at the heavenly realm she was departing. As her head turned, so did the chief's. When he did, his wife suddenly disappeared and he was alone. The chief then returned to the surface world on his own where he told his tribe the sad story of what he'd lost.

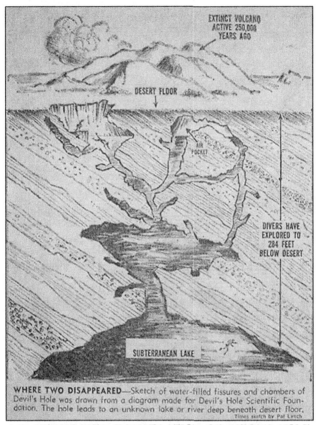

1965 NEWSPAPER ILLUSTRATION OF DEVIL'S HOLE. JIM HOUTZ COLLECTION.

Even people from the 20th Century believed in this underground world beneath Death Valley, among them Charles Manson. The famous cult leader had left San Francisco for Los Angeles in the late 1960s to come nearer to Death Valley, specifically Devil's Hole National Park, which he believed led to the underworld. Specifically, Manson wanted to start a race war that he codenamed "helter-skelter". Manson would then lead a selected group of whites into the desert where they would multiply in numbers. They would then escape into the underworld, which Manson believed the gateway to was located in Death Valley in the form of Devil's Hole National Park. Beneath that, he would find a sea of gold which was rumored to exist by the Native American population, along with the proverbial land full of milk and honey, a tree that bore 12 different kinds of fruit and which was bathed in eternal light via glowing walls. Furthermore, Manson believed there were already people waiting for him in the underworld. Of course, Manson was arrested before he could make his journey into the underworld but reports do say that he and his followers spent days and days in the heat of Death Valley looking for the entrance in 1968. Some think that Manson learned of the existence of this underworld through the tales of a prospector identified only as White.

In the 1920s, White may have found the mythical underground kingdom, or at least the basis for the myth. According to the tale, White was looking through an old abandoned mine at Wingate Pass in the southwest corner of Death Valley. Suddenly, the floor collapsed and he fell into an underground tunnel. With no other choice, White explored the labyrinth before him and eventually stumbled upon a catacomb of mummies. According to White, there were hundreds of them, all clad in leather and surrounded by gold bars and other treasures. Odder yet, White saw a tunnel that was lit by a pale, green and yellow-tinted light. Afraid of the strange light source, he elected not to go towards it alone and, somehow, White made his way back to the surface. Eventually, he returned to the catacombs with his wife, and again later with another prospector identified as Fred Thomason.

White's bold claim was backed by a Paiute named Tom Wilson, a local guide and trapper in the area who claimed that his grandfather had discovered the catacombs many years ago. His story was mostly the same as White's, claiming that his grandfather wandered through miles and miles of tunnels. Only in the grandfather's case, the people in the underground city still lived. They were fair-skinned and wore leather-like clothing just as White described the mummies. They spoke in a tongue unknown to the Paiute, and curiously, they also had horses underground and an unknown food source he'd never seen on the surface. Lastly, he, too, backed the claims of the strange green-yellow illumination.

Upon returning to the surface, no one believed the man's far-out tale, which was why Wilson was happy to hear the account of White. Eventually, Wilson and White connected, and the latter agreed to lead a team of archeologists to the underground city. However, as is usual in these types of stories, White was unable to locate the exact entrance again despite having been there three times before.

Instead, they found only a dead-end tunnel carved through a section of solid rock. Wilson would then spend the rest of his life searching for the entrance.[21]

DEATH VALLEY BY ANSEL ADAMS.

While that may put a dampener on the legend of the lost city, in 1932, yet another similar tale emerged in the book *Death Valley Men* by Bourke Lee, an old area prospector. He, too, told of an underground city, this one located in the Panamint Mountains of Death Valley. According to Lee, two men identified only as Bill and Jack were exploring the area of Wingate Pass. The ground suddenly collapsed and they fell into an old mine shaft and from there followed it for 20 miles into the heart of the Panamint Mountains.

---

[21] He passed away in 1968.

In the men's own words, which appear in *Death Valley Men*, they described it as a "city thousands of-years-old and worth billions of dollars!"[22]

The underground city they found sounded very similar to the one described by White. If it wasn't the same one, then it must've been a sister city. They found mummies within the city that they said wore large armbands and carried golden spears. There were also treasure chambers within stone vaults full of gold bars and statues, along with precious gemstones.

More interesting were their descriptions of the stone city's mechanics, as they claimed that huge doors in the city were operated by a series of counterweights. They also claimed to see huge stone wheelbarrows.

> I saw some doors cut in the solid rock of the walls. The doors are big slabs of rock on hinges you can't see. A big rock bar lets down across them. I tried to lift up the bars and couldn't move them. I fooled around trying to get the doors open. It must have been an hour before I took hold of a little latch like on the short end of the bar and the great big bar swung up. These people knew about counterweights and all those great big rock doors with their barlocks— they must weigh hundreds of tons— are all balanced so you can move them with your little finger, if you find the right place.[23]

---

[22] Reprinted in *Lost Cities & Ancient Mysteries of the Southwest*, p.470.
[23] Ibid, p.472.

The men claimed the city was illuminated by a series of lights generated by underground gasses. Of the city's lighting methods, the men explained,

...these old people had a natural gas they used for lighting and cooking. I found it by accident. I was bumping around in the dark. Everything was hard and cold and I kept thinking I was seeing people and I was pretty scared. I stumbled over something on the floor and fell down. Before I could get up there was a little explosion and gas flames all around the room lighted up. What I fell over was the rock lever that turned on the gas, and my candle set the gas off. Then was when I saw all the men, and the polished table, and the big statue.[24]

The two men grabbed all the treasure they could carry and then found an exit tunnel leading upwards and out halfway up the eastern slope of the Panamint Mountains:

It leads all through a great underground city; through the treasure vaults, the royal palace and the council chambers; and a connects to a series of beautiful galleries with stone arches in the East slope of the Panamint Mountains. Those arches are like great big windows in the side of the mountain and they look down on Death Valley. They are high above the valley now, but we believe that those entrances in the

[24] Ibid, 471-472.

mountainside were used by the ancient people that built the city. They used to land their boats there.[25]

That's right; the two men believed that the valley was once part of a series of lakes and that the arched openings were ancient docs for sea vessels.

Sadly, similar to the conclusion of White's tale, when the men tried to find the entrance a second time, they failed.[26] Not only that, the treasure they had carried out was stolen. According to the two men in *Death Valley Men*, "One government man said he'd like to see the stuff and we went back to our friend to get the gold and jewels and he told us he never seen them; and dared us to try and get them back. You see, he double-crossed us."[27]

So, in the end, they had no proof of their fantastic tale. Ultimately, the two men disappeared on one of their expeditions into the mountains to find the exit they had used.

Another believer in a lost underground city of riches in the area was the enigmatic Death Valley Scotty. Walter Scott, a.k.a. "Death Valley Scotty," was certainly a mystery to those who knew him. No one knew exactly where he amassed his wealth, but clearly he had some, for eventually he built a luxurious castle in the middle of the desert that still stands to this day. Furthermore, whenever Scotty

---

[25] Ibid, pp.470-471.

[26] They claimed that a rainstorm had altered the terrain too much to find it.

[27] Reprinted in *Lost Cities & Ancient Mysteries of the Southwest*, p.473.

would become low on funds, he would disappear into the desert and suddenly return wealthy again. Tales of the underground city were told almost every night at his castle to thrill the guests. The only direct correlation between Scotty and the treasure can be found in the book *Death Valley Men* where Scotty more or less says admits he knows exactly where the city is even though he doesn't reveal the location to the reader.

POSTCARD SHOWING SCOTTY'S CASTLE.

Then, in the late 1940s came one of the most publicized accounts of the lost city yet. Appearing in the *Butte Montana Standard* on August 5, 1947, was the following:

Ancient Relics Uncovered in Desert Area

LOS ANGELES. Aug. 4.—[UP]— A retired Ohio doctor has discovered relics of an ancient civilization, whose men were eight or nine feet tall, in the Colorado desert near the Arizona-Nevada-California line, an associate said Monday.

Howard E. Hill of Los Angeles speaking before the Transportation club, disclosed that several well-preserved mummies were taken Sunday from caverns in an area roughly 180 miles square extending through much of southern Nevada from Death Valley. Calif., across the Colorado river into Arizona.

Hill said the discoverer is Dr. F. Bruce Russell, retired Cincinnati physician, who stumbled on the first of several tunnels in 1931, shortly after going West and deciding to try mining for his health.

Not until this year, however, did Dr. Russell go into the situation thoroughly. Hill told the luncheon with Dr. Daniel S. Bovee of Los Angeles — who, with his father, helped open up New Mexico's cliff dwellings—Dr. Russell has found mummified remains together with implements of the civilization, which Dr. Bovee had tentatively placed at about 80,000 years ago.

"These giants are clothed in garments consisting of a medium length jacket and troupers extending slightly below the knees," said Hill.

"The texture of the material is said to resemble gray dyed sheepskin, but obviously it was taken from an animal unknown today."

Then, appearing in the *Valparaiso Vidette Messenger* on August 5, 1947, was this story:

MUMMIES OF THE AMERICAS

Group Claims Discovery of Early Giants

By PATRICIA CLARY
(United Press Staff Correspondent)
LOS ANGELES. Aug. 5.—(UP) — A band of amateur archeologists announced today that they have discovered a lost civilization of men nine feet tall in California caverns.

Howard E. Hill, spokesman for the expedition, said the civilization may be "the fabled lost continent of Atlantis."

The caves contain mummies of men and animals and implements of a culture 80,000 years old but "in some respects more advanced than ours," Hill said.

He said the 32 caves covered a 180-square-mile area in California's Death Valley and southern Nevada.

"This discovery may be more important than the unveiling of King Tut's tomb," he said.

Professionals Skeptical

Professional archaeologists were skeptical of Hill's story. Los Angeles county museum scientists pointed out that dinosaurs and tigers. which Hill said lay side by side in the caves, appeared on earth 10,000,000 to 15,000,000 years apart.

Hill said the caves were discovered in 1931 by Dr. P. Bruce Russell, Beverly Hills physician, who literally fell in while sinking a shaft for a mining claim.

Russell and several hobbyists incorporated after the war as Amazing Explorations, Inc., and started digging.

Several caverns contained mummied remains of "a race of men eight to nine feet tall." Hill said they apparently wore a prehistoric zoot suit—a hair garment of medium length jacket and knee length trousers.

Find Ritual Hall

Another cavern contained their ritual hall with devices and markings similar to the Masonic order, he said.

A long tunnel from this temple took the party into a room where Hill said, well-preserved remains of dinosaurs, saber-toothed tigers, imperial elephants and other extinct beasts were paired off in niches as if on display.

"Some catastrophe" apparently drove the people into the caves, he said. All of the implements of their civilization were found, he said, including household utensils and stoves which apparently cooked by radio waves.

"I know," he said, "that you won't believe that."

Unfortunately, there's not much in the way of follow-ups to the article. For instance, Dr. Russell died not long after the article's publication when his car was found abandoned with a busted radiator in a remote region of Death Valley. To quote from Mike Marinacci's book *Mysterious California*, "The desert can be very deceiving to anyone not used to traveling it. Months later Russell's car was found abandoned, with a burst radiator, in a remote area of Death Valley. His suitcase was still in the car."

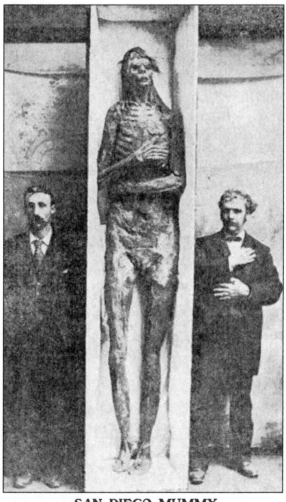

SAN DIEGO MUMMY.

However, these weren't the only mummies discovered in Death Valley or California in general. In 1898, H. Flagler Cowden and his brother Charles were conducting an archaeological dig in Death Valley when they uncovered the skeletal remains of a woman seven and a half feet tall. In the same strata that she was found were also discovered the remains of ice age creatures like prehistoric camels and possibly woolly mammoths and even petrified palm trees and other plant life.[28] Odder yet, the mummy appeared to have possessed what may have once been a tale! Three years before that discovery, in July of 1895, a group of miners working in the vicinity of Bridal Veil Falls found yet another giant woman who was just four inches shy of being seven feet tall.

Today, the area of the alleged underground city near Wingate Pass is part of the China Lake Naval Weapons Center and is closed to the public. Coincidence? The story is a bit similar to one where the U.S. military just happened to acquire the site of a similar underground treasure cache at Victorio Peak in what is now White Sands Missile Range in New Mexico. David Hatcher Childress wondered the same thing in his book *Lost Cities & Ancient Mysteries of the Southwest,* where he surmised,

---

[28] The discovery of the remains of lush vegetation almost lends credence to the earlier legend recounted at the beginning of the chapter.

Is it possible that the government did indeed become very interested in the underground catacombs of Death Valley? The southwestern portion of Death Valley around Wingate Pass did, in fact, become part of the China Lake Naval Weapons Center. Had the government possibly explored the Wingate Pass underground passages themselves and then decided to take the area over?"[29]

Sources:

Childress, David Hatcher. *Lost Cities and Ancient Mysteries of the Southwest.* Adventures Unlimited Press, 2009.

Kathy Weiser-Alexander. "The Hidden City of Death Valley." Legends of America. (August 2021)
https://www.legendsofamerica.com/ca-deathvalleyundergroundcity/

---

[29] Childress, *Lost Cities & Ancient Mysteries of the Southwest*, pp.474-475.

THE MARTINDALE MUMMIES

On July 30, 1899, the *Plain Dealer* reported on some more giant, noteworthy mummies unearthed in California.

MUMMIES FOUND IN A CAVE

Remains of a Woman Seven Feet Six Inches Tall and Her Child Discovered Wrapped in Parchment

Scientists of the West are greatly interested in the mummified remains of a woman, supposed to have belonged to a prehistoric race, found in a cave in the Yosemite Valley, in Southern California, and now in the possession of the Kansas State Historical Society, at Topeka, Kan. It was found by G.F. Martindale, of Scranton, Kan., who, with a party of friends, was out in the Yosemite Valley on a pleasure expedition.

The discovery was made quite by accident. The members of the party were in a ravine and were resting from their exertions. One of the party began prying up the stones along the side of the ravine, which was covered with moss and grass. A hole was discovered, and upon further investigation a hermetically sealed cave of large dimensions was revealed.

It was in this cave that the mummified remains of the woman were found. Mr. Martindale says that the cave was evidently sealed up by a race of people at so remote a period that the accumulation of years of deposits had destroyed all signs of the existence of the cave.

The woman evidently belonged to a race long since extinct. The mummy measures seven feet six inches in height and has many characteristics not possessed by any race of people now known. Scientists and students of archaeology in Kansas are greatly puzzled over what niche in the world's history to place this woman. Some even go so far as to express the belief that she was full grown before Adam ever saw the light of day.

While this may seem an exaggerated statement, says the New York Herald, yet it must be remembered that Augustus Le Plongeon, in his work entitled "Sacred Mysteries Among the Mayas and Quiches," traces the origin of the human race back 11,500 years to a race of people which he locates in Central America and southern Mexico, which is contiguous territory to that in which this mummy was found.

Le Plongeon locates this race by investigations among the antique palaces and temples of the Mayas and by interpretation of passages of the Troano manuscript, which was evidently left by some of the priests of the race. The history and civilization of this tribe was very similar to that of Greek mythology, and the latter has the appearance of having been copied to a certain extent from the Mayas.

The existence of a prehistoric race in this section of the country is further borne out by the discovery made a few years ago by the well-known Mexican archaeologist, Signor S. Marghieri. In a cave on the east side of the Sierra Madre mountains, about two hundred miles of Deming, in old Mexico, he found the mummified remains of four beings, evidently father, mother and two children. The mummies were wrapped in a textile resembling the tanned hide of an animal, and were well preserved. They are now in the museum of the State Mining society of California.

When found the Kansas mummy was lying on its back on the floor of the cave and in its arms an infant was clasped. Both the mother and child are in a high state of preservation. They were wrapped with a thin material resembling parchment, but probably animals' hide. The mother's hair is jet black. Her teeth, finger nails, and, in fact, all portions of the body are perfect, with the exception of abnormal size. The foot is about square in front. In other words, the tops are all about the same length. This is the same shaped foot found by Le Plongeon to have belonged to the tribe which existed near the Pacific coast thousands of years before the time of Adam.

The mummy was brought from California to Kansas in a long box, somewhat resembling a coffin. It was presented to the Kansas State Historical society by Mr. Martindale, and has since been viewed by numerous scientists and archaeologists from various parts of the west. I had the box placed in an upright position and photographed, as is shown by the accompanying picture. The man standing beside the picture is Mr. J.J. Mickey, clerk of the Kansas state railroad board. He is a man of about the average hight. His picture was taken for the purpose of showing by comparison, the great high of the mummy.

Prof. Winslow Anderson, who, in connection with William Irelan, state mineralogist of California, made an investigation of the mummies heretofore mentioned, and the caves in which they were found, has an exhaustive treatise on the origin of the ancient tribes of the Pacific coast in the report of the state mining bureau of California, 1888 to 1896. He finds that the Maya or Quiche empire was in a high state of civilization at the dawn of the Christian era. He deduces the conclusion that the origin of this race of people dates back many thousand years before the Christian era.

CHAPTER 15
BILLY THE KIDS PICKLED TRIGGER FINGER

No outlaw's life after death can compete with that of William H. Bonney, alias Billy the Kid. While it's true that both Butch Cassidy and Jesse James were said to escape death's clutches—at least as far as the accepted historical record goes—Billy the Kid's life after death is truly unequaled. Not only did he have nearly a dozen men claiming to be him after his death in 1881, but his grave markers have also been stolen nearly a half dozen times as well!

Much of what is known of the Kid can be attributed to legend over fact, including his birthdate of November 23, 1859 (which is also conveniently the birthday of his first biographer, Ash Upson). The Kid led a rough life, losing his mother in Silver City, New Mexico, to tuberculosis at the age of fifteen in 1874. After that began his life of what some call crime and others just call survival in the Wild West. He was forced to kill a man in self defense in Arizona and migrated back to New Mexico not long after. There he found himself embroiled in the bloody Lincoln County range war of 1878. After this, Billy relied on rustling cattle to get by and was gunned down by Sheriff Pat Garrett in Fort Sumner in July of 1881... allegedly.

THE KID'S FOOTSTONE RETURNED TO FORT SUMNER.

Tall tales exist that either Garrett shot the wrong man or conspired with the Kid to let him escape, but we won't go down that rabbit hole here. Besides, firmer evidence seems to suggest that the Kid was laid to rest in the Old Fort Sumner Cemetery. However, I use the term rest loosely, for only a year after being planted in the ground, his grave marker, a crude wooden cross made of

fenceposts, was stolen by his ex-girlfriend, Paulita
Maxwell.

BILLY THE KID, THE BOY BANDIT KING.

Paulita and her brother Pete had a $10 wager
going that she would be too afraid to go out to

Billy's grave at midnight due to Billy's ghost. When Paulita agreed to make the short journey to the cemetery, Pete insisted that she bring back a weed or flower to prove she had been there, only she brought back the entire cross to her doubting brother. The next morning Paulita sent one of the servants to put the cross back into the ground. As it turned out, Paulita begat a tradition of stealing Billy's marker. Years later, the crude wooden cross would be stolen away to New England. When it was replaced many years later by a nice footstone, it was stolen in 1950 and not recovered until 1976! It was stolen again in 1981 and recovered within a week. After that, the footstone was literally shackled to the gravesite, and a jail cell was built around the burial plot.

More macabre than the theft of Billy's markers is the alleged theft of his bones themselves. The first story regarding the mutilation of the Kid's body appeared in the July 25, 1881, edition of the *Las Vegas Optic* in their now infamous "The Fatal Finger" story:

An esteemed friend of the *Optic* at Fort Sumner, L.W. Hale, has sent us the index finger of "Billy, the Kid," the one which has snapped many a man's life into eternity. It is well preserved in alcohol and has been viewed by many in our office today. If the rush continues we shall purchase a small tent and open a side show to which complementary tickets will be issued to our personal friends.[30]

Though for many years this story was thought to be a hoax, professor emeritus Robert J. Stahl wrote a lengthy piece on the trigger finger for *True West* magazine. Stahl clarified that people actually did trek to the *Optic* office to see a finger in a jar. Whether it was really Billy's or not is unknown, but reportedly they were allowed to gaze upon it so long as they paid $3 for a yearlong subscription to the paper!

As it turned out, the mysterious donor, L.W. Hale, was a real New Mexico resident and a first class peddler. A relative once said of him, "He was a wheeler and dealer, but always an honest and fair wheeler and dealer."[31] The family also confirmed Hale was indeed in the Ft. Sumner area at the time of the Kid's death and was a friend of *Optic* editor Russell A. Kistler.

An even more macabre story appeared in the *Optic* on September 10th entitled "The Kid Kidnapped" and read:

The fifth day after the burial of the notorious young desperado, a fearless skelologist of this county, whose name, for substantial reasons, cannot be divulged, proceeded to Sumner, and

---

[30] *Billy the Kid: Las Vegas Newspaper Accounts Of His Career, 1880-1881.*

[31] Stahl, "Lower William Hale and Joshua Fred Hale," *Lincoln County, New Mexico Tells its Tales.*

in the silent watches of the night, with the assistance of a compadre, dug up the remains of the once mighty youth and carried them off in their wagon. The "stiff" was brought in to Las Vegas, arriving here at two o'clock in the morning, and was slipped quietly into the private office of a practical "sawbones," who, by dint of diligent labor and careful watching to prevent detection, boiled and scraped the skin off the "plate" so as to secure the skull, which was seen by a reporter last evening. The body, or remains proper, was covered in dirt in the corral, where it will remain until decomposition shall have robbed the frame of its meat, when the body will be dug up again and the skeleton "fixed up"—hung together by wires and varnished with shellac to make it presentable. Then the physicians will feel that their labors have been rewarded, for the skeleton of a crack frontiersman does not grow on every bush, and the "bones" of such men as the Kid are hard to find. The skull is already "dressed," and is considered quite a relic in itself. The index finger of the right hand, it will be remembered, was presented to THE OPTIC at the time the exhumation was made. As this member has been sent east, the skeleton now in process of consummation will not be complete in its fingers; but the loss is so trivial that it will be hardly noticeable.

According to Ft. Sumner resident Charles Foor, these newspaper articles caught the attention of Pat

Garrett. A 1928 article in the *Southwestern Dispatch* related that "Mr. For [sic] said that he had inspected the grave in the company of Pat Garrett 18 months after the internment and when the first claim of the moving of the bones was made by the Las Vegas people. At that time both men agreed that the grave was untouched."

One of Garrett's biographers, Richard O'Connor, claimed that Garret visited the grave several weeks later after his "indignation was aroused by reports that carnivals, dime museums, and other opportunistic enterprises were displaying what they claimed where parts of Billy's corpse." O'Connor also claimed that Garrett even dug up the body to make sure, but this is doubtful. Whatever the case, Garrett addressed the rumors in his book *Authentic Life of Billy the Kid*:

I said that the body was buried in the cemetery at Ft. Sumner. I wish to add that it is there today intact—skull, fingers, toes, bones, and every hair on the head that was buried with the body on that 15th of July, doctors, newspaper editors, and paragraphers to the contrary now withstanding. Some presuming swindlers have claimed to have the Kid's skull on exhibition, or one of his fingers, or some other portion of his body, and one medical gentleman has persuaded credulous idiots that he has all the bones strung up on wires...Again I say the Kid's body lies undisturbed in the grave—and I speak of what I know.

The saga of Billy's body parts continued on September 19, when the *Optic* received a letter from a woman, Kate Tenney of Oakland, California, alleging to be the Kid's ex-lover requesting that she be given the notorious trigger finger. The editor then replied to the woman that it had already been sold for $150. The editor went on to joke that perhaps the sawbones who had Billy's corpse from the September 10th story could send the poor girl "a shank bone—or something of that kind." While the *Optic* editor, Russell Kistler, is usually attributed to cooking up the letter, this story was actually run by another editor at the *Optic*, Lute Wilcox. The finger was supposedly sold to one Albert Kunz, who operated a drug store in Las Vegas. Kistler wrote of Kunz's departure to Waterville, Kansas, and indeed the *Waterville Telegraph* reported on September 16th that "Mr. Albert Kunz returned home last Monday from Las Vegas. He is looking hale and hearty, and brought as a relic of barbarism a specimen of the physical existence of Billy the Kid."[32]

The *Optic* kept up its coverage of Billy's traveling finger in their October 14th issue, where it was reported that it was now on display in Indiana at several county fairs. This was the last item to be reported on the finger's whereabouts, and it is presumed to be lost. Thanks to the 'Fatal Finger' story, readership to the *Optic* soared, so other

---

[32] Stahl, "The Mysterious Journey of Billy the Kid's Trigger Finger," *True West*.

newspapers began to follow suit. In 1885 the *Silver City Enterprise* wrote a story on the Kid's skull being in the possession of an Albuquerque man.

Despite those claims, most likely Billy's bones still rest under the Fort Sumner ground, as evidenced by a few sightings of the Kid's ghost. Of the old cemetery, Charlie Foor said in Walter Noble Burns' *Saga of Billy the Kid* that "They say it's haunted. Some folks'll drive a mile out of their way at night to keep from passin' it." Burns gave a characteristic vivid description of the Kid's grave, then a barren patch of land devoid of a proper marker:

The bare space is perhaps the length of a man's body. Salt grass grows in a mat all around it, but queerly enough stops short at the edges and not a blade sprouts upon it. A Spanish gourd vine with ghostly gray pointed leaves stretches its trailing length toward the blighted spot but, within a few inches of its margin, veers sharply off to one side as if with conscious purpose to avoid contagion. Perfectly bare the space is except for a shoot of prickly pear that crawls across it like a green snake; a gnarled bristly, heat cursed desert cactus crawling like a snake across the heart of Billy the Kid. "It's always bare like this," says Old Man Foor, standing back from this spot as if half-afraid of some inexplicable contamination. "I don't know why. Grass or nothin' else will grow on it—that's all. You might almost think there's poison in the ground."

THE OLD BILLY THE KID CURIO SHOP.

Foor even suggested that cracks in the hard dry earth made out the picture of a skeletal hand reaching out from certain angles. Burns went on to concur, perhaps merely for the delight of his readers, that he too saw "the sun-drawn skiagraph" that somehow stretched from the grave.

Saga also included a brief comical episode on the Maxwell family involving the Kid's ghost shortly after his death in the chapter "The Belle of Old Fort Sumner." One night Paulita and Pete Maxwell with a neighbor, Manuel Abreu, were sitting inside when they heard the sound of soft footsteps walking across the front porch as if someone were creeping along in their stalking feet. "Can it be that the Kid has come back from the dead?" an excited Abreu asked. Pete Maxwell chimed in and remarked, "Every night since his death I've heard queer noises about the old house." Paulita was the voice of reason among the men, who were perhaps just trying to scare her, and chided them for their foolishness. "But Paulita, they say the spirits of murdered men return to haunt the place where they were killed," Abreu continued. The footsteps began again and Maxwell crossed himself, "Billy the Kid's ghost!" Finally having enough, Paulita went outside to investigate only to find it was merely a jackrabbit. It is reported in other stories that Pete really did fear the ghost of Billy, for when it came time to sell his ranch a short time later to the New England Cattle Company, Maxwell insisted he could not sell Billy's favorite horse, Don, or "Billy, dead these three years, would rise up in his grave and curse me."[33] Likewise, Deluvina Maxwell, a close friend of the Kid's, was herself wildly superstitious and would not pass the cemetery after dark, claiming to have seen the ghost of a buffalo soldier there once, but never Billy.

An old *True West* article by artist Lea F. McCarty relating his trek to Fort Sumner to find a picture of the Kid's funeral mentions tales of Billy's ghost several times but fails to go into detail on them. The closest the article gets to a bonafide Billy ghost sighting comes from a conversation between McCarty and Tom Sullivan, a clerk at the Billy the Kid Curio Shop near the grave. McCarty asked why the property owner never sold the cemetery to the state, to which Sullivan replied, "They don't want it." He then leaned in close to elaborate:

---

[33] Kadlec, *They "Knew" Billy the Kid*, 122.

He bent over to whisper with the wind howling outside..."Some say [the owner] is afeard of Billy's ghost. It's been seen, you know, by some of the folks around here. Mr. Austin saw it, so he says, riding one night across the old fort ruins and carrying the wooden cross. He rode the beautiful grey he was so proud of. *Duerme bien querido.*"

The Spanish phrase whispered by Sullivan at the end was the inscription "Rest in peace, beloved" said to be on the original cross. When Sullivan went on to recount the poor long gone cross's elaborate history, he mentioned how Paulita Maxwell once stole it to win a bet. "That wouldn't have been me sir! I've seen Billy's ghost myself, but I don't expect you to believe it!"

Sources:

Carson, Kit. "Billy the Kid's Restless Bones." *Real West* (March 1962).

Kadlec, Robert F. Ed. *They "Knew" Billy the Kid.* Ancient City Press, 1987.

McCarty, Lea F. "Why is it so important that theirs is a photograph of Billy the Kid's Funeral?" *True West* (November-December 1960)

Stahl, Robert J. "The Mysterious Journey of Billy the Kid's Trigger Finger." *True West* (July 2013).

CHAPTER 16
THE MINIATURE MUMMY

One hot summer day in July of 1934, a remarkable discovery was made in the San Pedro Mountains. Two prospectors, Cecil Main and Frank Carr, were mining for gold in the hills. While tracing a seam of gold into the rock face of the mountain, they ran into a literal dead end. They had no choice but to blast into the rock face. To their disappointment, when the smoke cleared, they found no more gold. However, the explosion had revealed a hidden cave. The little cavern measured four feet wide and fifteen feet long. Sitting cross-legged on a ledge, they found a tiny mummy only six inches tall. It had been mummified from the natural elements over time, and as such most of its features were still intact and discernable. And what strange features they were. A gelatinous substance covered the head, and the facial features were odd, with a low, flat forehead and flattened nose. Then there were the rather bulbous eyes and the full set of teeth—I point out the teeth because if the tiny six-inch mummy was a fetus, as some argue, then it shouldn't have had teeth.

> **MUMMIFIED PYGMY FOUND**
> LUSK, Wyo.—(U.P)—A mummified pygmy, believed by scientists to be a progenitor of the present human race, was exhibited in Lusk recently. The mummy is owned by Homer F. Sherrill, of Crawford, Neb., and has baffled scientists in various parts of the country where it has been sent for classification. It was unearthed in a cave on a slope of one of the Peaks of Pedro mountain, near Casper, Wyo.

ARTICLE ABOUT THE 1932 SAN PEDRO MUMMY.

Though they were still disappointed by the lack of gold, Main and Carr knew they could still make a profit off of the mummy in exhibitions. After all, around this same time, the mummified carcass of the man alleged to be John Wilkes Booth was a popular attraction at carnivals and circuses. So it certainly wasn't unusual in the era for curiosities such as that to hit the road or be part of a traveling cabinet of curiosities.

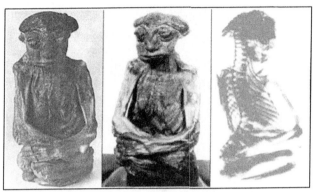

THE 1932 SAN PEDRO MUMMY.

Due to being found in the San Pedro Mountains, they nicknamed their little mummy Pedro and took him to Casper, Wyoming, about 60 miles away. It's unknown if Main and Carr exhibited the carcass themselves, or if they sold it right away to a carnival barker, but it for certain toured around Wyoming for two years up until 1936. After that, it was purchased by Meeteetse drug store owner Floyd Jones, who put the mummy in his display window to entice customers to come inside.

Later, Pedro made his way back to Casper and into the sales room of a car dealership owned by Ivan Goodman. With a flare for showmanship, he touted that, "It's educational! It's Scientific! It will amaze and thrill you. It's a pygmy preserved as it actually lived!" Goodman made up a story that the mummy was thousands of years old and a distant ancestor of the human race.

Little Pedro would seem to have died a violent death unbefitting of a little baby, as his skull appeared to have been smashed along with a broken collarbone and a damaged spine. Of course, it could have been an accident, but it's possible that Pedro was actually a member of a mythical, war-like race of little people known as the Nimerigar.

This race of little people was said to live in the vicinity of Wind River and the San Pedro Mountains. According to myth, the Nimerigar stood anywhere between 20 inches and three feet in height. Despite their short stature, the Nimerigar were not to be trifled with, as they were not only violent but also had magic powers. The Nez Perce tribe alleged that the beings could turn themselves invisible with a special grass, for example. The Shoshone considered the little people to be tricksters and blamed most of their bad luck on them. Similar to the Nimerigar was another tribe called the Nirumbee, which would sometimes abduct children. The violent aspect of the Nimerigar would seem to fit in with Pedro's brutal death, as it was said that the Nimerigar would kill the elderly with a blow to the skull when they outlived their usefulness.

Pedro was at one point x-rayed by the American Museum of Natural History in New York, and these x-rays were later verified by the Anthropology Department of Harvard University. Though the results proved that Pedro was an actual mummy and not a cobbled-together hoax, the question still remained: what was it? Of course, no one from that era would stop to propose it may have come from a mystical race of little people. As far as scientists were concerned, Pedro must have been a baby suffering from a rare genetic condition known as anencephaly. The unfortunate condition occurs in the womb and often results in the absence of part of the fetus's brain, skull, and scalp, which seemed to match Pedro's case.

You may now be asking why proper testing hasn't been conducted on Pedro since then? That's because Pedro mysteriously disappeared in the 1950s. It is thought that Goodman, the car salesman, sold him to what some call a "New York con man." According to David Weatherly in *Monsters of Big Sky Country*, the New York man was named Leonard Walder, and the mummy unfortunately vanished upon Walder's death in the 1980s.

LOST EGYPTIAN CITY OF THE GRAND CANYON

Since this series has a tradition of ending on a significant location, no other place seems more appropriate to conclude our journey than the alleged lost Egyptian city in the Grand Canyon. If an old newspaper article is to be believed, it would seem that an Egyptian ship sailed across the ocean to come all the way to Arizona thousands of years ago. And when they did so, they apparently left an Egyptian tomb in the Grand Canyon itself, not dissimilar to the Valley of Kings near Luxor, Egypt. Actually, it wasn't just a tomb; it was practically a whole necropolis full of ancient mummies. True or not, the fantastic tale was first printed on April 5, 1909, in the *Arizona Gazette*.

Oldest Paper in Phoenix—Twenty-Ninth Year.

EXPLORATIONS IN GRAND CANYON

Mysteries of Immense Rich Cavern Being Brought to Light.

JORDAN IS ENTHUSED

Remarkable Finds Indicate Ancient People Migrated From Orient.

The latest news of the progress of the explorations of what is now regarded by scientists as not only the oldest archaeological discovery in the United States, but one of the most valuable in the world, which was mentioned some time ago in the Gazette, was brought to the city yesterday by G. E. Kinkaid, the explorer who found the great underground citadel of the Grand Canyon during a trip from Green river, Wyoming, down the Colorado, in a wooden boat, to Yuma, several months ago. According to the story related yesterday to the Gazette by Mr. Kinkaid, the archaeologists of the Smithsonian Institute, which is financing the explorations, have made discoveries which almost conclusively prove that the race which inhabited this mysterious cavern, hewn in solid rock by human hands, was of oriental origin, possibly from Egypt, tracing back to Ramses. If their theories are borne out by the translation of the tablets engraved with hieroglyphics, the mystery of the prehistoric peoples of North America, their ancient arts, who they were and whence they came, will be solved. Egypt and the Nile, and Arizona and the Colorado will be linked by a historical chain running back to ages which staggers the wildest fancy of the fictionist.

A Thorough Investigation.

Under the direction of Prof. S. A. Jordan, the Smithsonian Institute is now prosecuting the most thorough explorations, which will be continued until the last link in the chain is forged. Nearly a mile underground, about 1480 feet below the surface, the long main

perfect ventilation of the cavern, the steady draught that blows through, indicates that it has another outlet to the surface.

Mr. Kinkaid's Report.

Mr. Kinkaid was the first white child born in Idaho and has been an explorer and hunter all his life, thirty years having been in the service of the Smithsonian Institute. Even briefly recounted, his history sounds fabulous, almost grotesque.

"First, I would impress that the cavern is nearly inaccessible. The entrance is 1486 feet down the sheer canyon wall. It is located on government land and no visitor will be allowed there under penalty of trespass. The scientists wish to work unmolested, without fear of the archaeological discoveries being disturbed by curio or relic hunters. A trip there would be fruitless, and the visitor would be sent on his way. The story of how I found the cavern has been related, but in a paragraph: I was journeying down the Colorado river in a boat, alone, looking for mineral. Some forty-two miles up the river from the El Tovar Crystal canyon I saw on the east wall, stains in the sedimentary formation about 2000 feet above the river bed. There was no trail to this point, but I finally reached it with great difficulty. Above a shelf which hid it from view from the river, was the mouth of the cave. There are steps leading from this entrance some thirty yards to what was, at the time the cavern was inhabited, the level of the river. When I saw the chisel marks on the wall inside the entrance, I became interested, secured my gun and went in. During that trip I went back several hundred feet along the main passage, till I came to the crypt in which I discovered the mummies. One of these I stood up and photographed by flashlight. I gathered a number of relics, which I carried down the Colorado to Yuma, from whence I shipped them to Washington with details of the discovery. Following this, the explorations were undertaken.

The Passages.

"The main passageway is about 12 feet wide, narrowing to 5 feet toward the farther end. About 57 feet from the entrance, the first side-passages branch off to the right and left, along which, on both sides, are a number of rooms about the size of ordinary living rooms of today, though some are 30 or 40 feet square. These are entered by oval-shaped doors and are ventilated by round air spaces through the walls into the passages. The walls are about 3 feet 6 inches in thickness. The passages are chiseled or hewn as straight as could be laid out by an engineer. The ceilings of many of the rooms converge to a center. The side-passages near the entrance run at a sharp angle from the main hall, but toward the rear they gradually reach a right angle in direction.

The Shrine.

"Over a hundred feet from the entrance is the cross-hall, several hundred feet long, in which was found the idol, or image, of the people's god, sitting cross-legged, with a lotus flower or lily in each hand. The east of the

CREEPY CADAVERS, OUTLAW MUMMIES, AND LOST CITIES OF THE DEAD

Explorations in Grand Canyon

Mysteries of Immense Rich Cavern Being Brought to Light Remarkable finds indicate ancient people migrated from Orient as edited by The Arizona Gazette

March 12, 1909

The latest news of the progress of the explorations of what is now regarded by scientists as not only the oldest archaeological discovery in the United States, but one of the most valuable in the world, which was mentioned some time ago in the Gazette, was brought to the city yesterday by G. E. Kinkaid, the explorer who found the great underground citadel of the Grand Canyon during a trip from Green River, Wyoming, down the Colorado, in a wooden boat, to Yuma, several months ago.

According to the story related to the Gazette by Mr. Kinkaid, the archaeologists of the Smithsonian Institute, which is financing the expeditions, have made discoveries which almost conclusively prove that the race which inhabited this mysterious cavern, hewn in solid rock by human hands, was of oriental origin, possibly from Egypt, tracing back to Ramses.

If their theories are borne out by the translation of the tablets engraved with hieroglyphics, the mystery of the prehistoric peoples of North America, their ancient arts, who they were and whence they came, will be solved.

Egypt and the Nile, and Arizona and the Colorado will be linked by a historical chain running back to ages which staggers the wildest fancy of the fictionist.

A Thorough Examination

Under the direction of Prof. S. A. Jordan, the Smithsonian Institute is now prosecuting the most thorough explorations, which will be continued until the last link in the chain is forged.

Nearly a mile long tunnel underground, about 1480 feet below the surface, the long main passage has been delved into, to find another mammoth chamber from which radiates scores of passageways, like the spokes of a wheel.

Several hundred rooms have been discovered, reached by passageways running from the main passage, one of them having been explored for 854 feet and another 634 feet.

The recent finds include articles which have never been known as native to this country, and doubtless they had their origin in the orient. War weapons, copper instruments, sharp-edged and hard as steel, indicate the high state of civilization reached by these strange people.

So interested have the scientists become that preparations are being made to equip the camp for extensive studies, and the force will be increased to thirty or forty persons.

"Before going further into the cavern, better facilities for lighting will have to be installed, for the darkness is dense and quite impenetrable for the average flashlight.

In order to avoid being lost, wires are being strung from the entrance to all passageways leading directly to large chambers. How far this cavern extends no one can guess, but it is now the belief of many that what has already been explored is merely the "barracks", to use an American term, for the soldiers, and that far into the under-world will be found the main communal dwellings of the families.

The perfect ventilation of the cavern, the steady draught that blows through, indicates that it has another outlet to the surface."

Mr. Kinkaid's Report

Mr. Kinkaid was the first white child born in Idaho and has been an explorer and hunter all his life, thirty years having been in the service of the Smithsonian Institute. Even briefly recounted, his history sounds fabulous, almost grotesque.

First, I would impress that the cavern is nearly inaccessible. The entrance is 1,486 feet down the sheer canyon wall. It is located on government land and no visitor will be allowed there under penalty of trespass.

The scientists wish to work unmolested, without fear of archaeological discoveries being disturbed by curios or relic hunters.

A trip there would be fruitless, and the visitor would be sent on his way. The story of how I found the cavern has been related, but in a paragraph: I was journeying down the Colorado river in a boat, alone, looking for mineral.

Some forty-two miles up the river from the El Tovar Crystal canyon, I saw on the east wall, stains in the sedimentary formation about 2,000 feet above the river bed. There was no trail to this point, but I finally reached it with great difficulty.

Above a shelf which hid it from view from the river, was the mouth of the cave. There are steps leading from this entrance some thirty yards to what was, at the time the cavern was inhabited, the level of the river.

When I saw the chisel marks on the wall inside the entrance, I became interested, securing my gun and went in. During that trip I went back several hundred feet along the main passage till I came to the crypt in which I discovered the mummies. One of these I stood up and photographed by flashlight. I gathered a number of relics, which I carried down the Colorado to Yuma, from whence I shipped them to Washington with details of the discovery.

Following this, the explorations were undertaken.

The Passages
The main passageway is about 12 feet wide, narrowing to nine feet toward the farther end.

About 57 feet from the entrance, the first side-passages branch off to the right and left, along which, on both sides, are a number of rooms about the size of ordinary living rooms of today, though some are 30 by 40 feet square. These are entered by oval-shaped doors and are ventilated by round air spaces through the walls into the passages. The walls are about three feet six inches in thickness.

The passages are chiseled or hewn as straight as could be laid out by an engineer.

The ceilings of many of the rooms converge to a center. The side-passages near the entrance run at a sharp angle from the main hall, but toward the rear they gradually reach a right angle in direction.

The Shrine

Over a hundred feet from the entrance is the cross-hall, several hundred feet long, in which are found the idol, or image, of the people's god, sitting cross-legged, with a lotus flower or lily in each hand. The cast of the face is oriental, and the carving this cavern. The idol almost resembles Buddha, though the scientists are not certain as to what religious worship it represents. Taking into consideration everything found thus far, it is possible that this worship most resembles the ancient people of Tibet. Surrounding this idol are smaller images, some very beautiful in form - others crooked-necked and distorted shapes, symbolical, probably, of good and evil. There are two large cactus with

179

protruding arms, one on each side of the dais on which the god squats. All this is carved out of hard rock resembling marble.

These people undoubtedly knew the lost art of hardening this metal, which has been sought by chemists for centuries without result. On a bench running around the workroom was some charcoal and other material probably used in the process.

There is also slag and stuff similar to matte, showing that these ancients smelted ores, but so far no trace of where or how this was done has been discovered, nor the origin of the ore. Among the other finds are vases or urns and cups of copper and gold, made very artistic in design. The pottery work includes enameled ware and glazed vessels.

Another passageway leads to granaries such as are found in the oriental temples. They contain seeds of various kinds. One very large storehouse has not yet been entered, as it is twelve feet high and can be reached only from above. Two copper hooks extend on the edge, which indicates that some sort of ladder was attached.

These granaries are rounded, as the materials of which they are constructed, I think, is a very hard cement. A gray metal is also found in this cavern, which puzzles the scientists, for its identity has not been established. It resembles platinum.

Strewn promiscuously over the floor everywhere are what people call 'cats eyes', a yellow stone of no great value. Each one is engraved with the head of the Malay type.

The Hieroglyphics

On all the urns, or walls over doorways, and tablets of stone which were found by the image are the mysterious hieroglyphics the key to which the Smithsonian Institute hopes yet to discover.

These writings resemble those on the rocks about this valley. The engraving on the tables probably has something to do with the religion of the people. Similar hieroglyphics have been found in the peninsula of Yucatan, but these are not the same as those found in the Orient.

Some believe these cave dwellers built the old canals in the Salt River Valley.

The Crypt

The tomb or crypt in which the mummies were found is one of the largest of the chambers, the walls slanting back at an angle of about 35 degrees. On these are tiers of mummies, each one occupying a separate hewn shelf. At the head of each is a small bench, on which is found copper cups and pieces of broken swords. Some of the mummies are covered with clay, and all are wrapped in a dark fabric.

The urns or cups on the lower tiers are crude, while as the higher shelves are reached, the urns are finer in design, showing a later stage of civilization. It is worthy of note that all the mummies examined so far have proved to be male, no children or females being buried here. This leads to the belief that this exterior section was the warriors' barracks.

Among the discoveries no bones of animals have been found, no skins, no clothing, no bedding. Many of the rooms are bare but for water vessels. One room, about 40 by 700 feet, was probably the main dining hall, for cooking utensils are found here. What these people lived on is a problem, though it is presumed that they came south in the winter and farmed in the valleys, going back north in the summer.

Upwards of 50,000 people could have lived in the caverns comfortably. One theory is that the present Indian tribes found in Arizona are descendants of the serfs or slaves of the people which inhabited the cave. Undoubtedly a good many thousands of years before the Christian era, a people lived here which reached a high stage of civilization.

The chronology of human history is full of gaps. Professor Jordan is much enthused over the discoveries and believes that the find will prove of incalculable value in archaeological work.

One thing I have not spoken of may be of interest. There is one chamber of the passageway to which is not ventilated, and when we approached it a deadly, snaky smell struck us. Our light would not penetrate the gloom, and until stronger ones are available we will not know what the chamber contains. Some say snakes, but other boo-hoo this idea and think it may contain a deadly gas or chemicals used by the ancients.

No sounds are heard, but it smells snaky just the same. The whole underground installation gives one of shaky nerves the creeps. The gloom is like a weight on one's shoulders, and our flashlights and candles only make the darkness blacker.

CAPE ROYAL GRAND CANYON BY ANSEL ADAMS.

Imagination can revel in conjectures and ungodly daydreams back through the ages that have elapsed till the mind reels dizzily in space.

An Indian Legend

In connection with this story, it is notable that among the Hopi Indians the tradition is told that their ancestors once lived in an underworld in the Grand Canyon till dissension arose between the good and the bad, the people of one heart and the people of two hearts.

Machetto, who was their chief, counseled them to leave the underworld, but there was no way out. The chief then caused a tree to grow up and pierce the roof of the underworld, and then the people of one heart climbed out. They tarried by Paisisvai (Red River), which is the Colorado, and grew grain and corn.

They sent out a message to the Temple of the Sun, asking the blessing of peace, good will and rain for people of one heart. That messenger never returned, but today at the Hopi villages at sundown can be seen the old men of the tribe out on the housetops gazing toward the sun, looking for the messenger.

When he returns, their lands and ancient dwelling place will be restored to them. That is the tradition.

Among the engravings of animals in the cave is seen the image of a heart over the spot where it is located. The legend was learned by W.E. Rollins, the artist, during a year spent with the Hopi Indians. There are two theories of the origin of the Egyptians. One is that they came from Asia another that the racial cradle was in the upper Nile region. Heeren, an Egyptologist, believed in the Indian origin of the Egyptians.

The discoveries in the Grand Canyon may throw further light on human evolution and prehistoric ages.

Thus ends the fantastic, Indiana Jones-like article. How well it holds up under scrutiny is debatable, and as always, there are pros and cons. As for the cons, though it's been rumored for years that the Smithsonian often covers up historical anomalies that don't fit the accepted timeline, what's more troubling in terms of this account are the identities of G.E. Kinkaid and S.A. Jordan. Contrary to what the article says, Idaho denies the claim that Kinkaid was the first white baby ever born there.

To circumvent the difficulties surrounding the identity of Kinkaid, David Hatcher Childress put forth a rather interesting theory in his book *Lost Cities & Ancient Mysteries of the Southwest*:

One interesting suggestion is that, while the discovery was real, the archaeologists might not have been. These men may not have been working for the Smithsonian out of Washington DC at all, but merely claiming to be doing so. This may have been a cover-up for an illegal archaeological dig that was raiding the ancient site and claiming legitimacy from a very distant, venerated institution. It may prove difficult, in 1909, to check on the credentials of the archaeologists, and there is no hint that anyone was actually trying to do this. These men may well have disappeared shortly after the article appeared, but not to Washington DC as we might suppose, but rather to San Francisco, Los Angeles, or Denver.[34]

---

[34] Childress, *Lost Cities & Ancient Mysteries*, pp.392-393.

The only thing really propping the story up is that the *Phoenix Gazette* did run a prior account of Kinkaid's journey down the Colorado on March 12, 1909. It ended by stating that "some interesting archaeological discoveries were unearthed and altogether the trip was of such interest that [Kinkaid] will repeat it next winter, in the company of friends."

Likewise, John Wesley Powell, a famous navigator of the Colorado River around 1870, corroborated some of Kinkaid's claims. In his book, *Exploration of the Colorado River and its Canyons* published in 1875, Powell hinted that he himself saw what looked to be large hollowed-out caves and suggestions of "architectural forms" while he was passing through Marble Canyon.

In the book, he wrote,

I walk down the gorge to the left at the foot of the cliff, climb to a bench, and discover a trail deeply worn into the rock. Where it crosses the side gulches in some places steps have been cut. I can see no evidence of its having been traveled for a long time. It was doubtless a path used by the people who inhabited this country anterior to the present Indian races – the people who built the communal houses of which mention has been made. I returned to camp about 3 o'clock and find that some of the men have discovered ruins and many fragments of pottery; also etchings and hieroglyphics on the rocks.

ANSEL ADAMS GRAND CANYON VIEW.

The last thing that the fantastic story has going for it is the odd Egyptian place names of the Grand Canyon, such as Cheops Pyramid and Isis Temple. Cheops Pyramid was one of many formations named by George Wharton James because he felt it resembled the same-named pyramid from Egypt. The name was officially recognized by the U.S. Board on Geographic Names in 1906, three years before the infamous story broke about the lost Egyptian City of the Grand Canyon. Ultimately, one can only wonder if the 1909 story was made up in response to these puzzling Egyptian names, or are they yet another clue in the mystery?

MUMMIES OF THE AMERICAS

Sources:

Childress, David Hatcher. *Lost Cities and Ancient Mysteries of the Southwest.* Adventures Unlimited Press, 2009.

INDEX

ABOUT THE AUTHOR

John LeMay was born and raised in Roswell, NM, the "UFO Capital of the World." He is the author of over 35 books on film and western history such as *Kong Unmade: The Lost Films of Skull Island, Tall Tales and Half Truths of Billy the Kid*, and *Roswell USA: Towns That Celebrate UFOs, Lake Monsters, Bigfoot and Other Weirdness.* In addition to non-fiction, he is also the author of the novel *The Noted Desperado Pancho Dumez.* He is also the editor/publisher of *The Lost Films Fanzine* and has written for magazines such as *True West, Cinema Retro*, and *Mad Scientist* to name only a few. He is a Past President of the Board of Directors for the Historical Society for Southeast New Mexico and the host of the web series *Roswell's Hidden History.*

THE BICEP BOOKS CATALOGUE

The following titles are available for purchase on Amazon.com, and are available to bookstores at a wholesale discount via Ingram Content Group (ISBNs of available editions listed for this purpose)

THE BIG BOOK OF JAPANESE GIANT MONSTER MOVIES SERIES

The third edition of the book that started it all! Reviews over 100 tokusatsu films between 1954 and 1988. All the Godzilla, Gamera, and Daimajin movies made during the Showa era are covered plus lesser known fare like *Invisible Man vs. The Human Fly* (1957) and *Conflagration* (1975). Softcover (380 pp/5.83" X 8.27") Suggested Retail: $19.99 SBN:978-1-7341546-4-1

This third edition reviews over 75 tokusatsu films between 1989 and 2019. All the Godzilla, Gamera, and Ultraman movies made during the Heisei era are covered plus independent films like *Reigo, King of the Sea Monsters* (2005), *Demeking, the Sea Monster* (2009) and *Attack of the Giant Teacher* (2019)! Softcover (260 pp/5.83" X 8.27") Suggested Retail: $19.99 ISBN: 978-1-7347816-4-9

This second edition of the Rondo Award nominated book covers un-produced monster scripts like *Bride of Godzilla* (1955), partially shot movies like *Giant Horde Beast Nezura* (1963), and banned films like *Prophecies of Nostradamus* (1974), plus hundreds of other lost productions. Softcover/Hard-cover (470pp. /7" X 10") Suggested Retail: $24.99 (sc)/$39.95(hc)ISBN: 978-1-73 41546-0-3 (hc)

This sequel to *The Lost Films* covers the non-giant monster unmade movie scripts from Japan such as *Frankenstein vs. the Human Vapor* (1963), *After Japan Sinks* (1974-76), plus lost movies like *Fearful Attack of the Flying Saucers* (1956) and *Venus Flytrap* (1968). Hardcover (200 pp/5.03" X 8.27")/Softcover (216 pp/ 5.5" X 8.5") Suggested Retail: $9.99 (sc)/$24.99(hc) ISBN:978-1-7341546 -3-4 (hc)

This companion book to *The Lost Films* charts the development of all the prominent Japanese monster movies including discarded screenplays, story ideas, and deleted scenes. Also includes bios for writers like Shinichi Sekizawa, Niisan Takahashi and many others. Comprehensive script listing and appendices as well. Hardcover/Softcover (370 pp./ 6"X9") Suggested Retail: $16.95(sc)/$34.99(hc)ISBN: 978-1-7341546-5-8 (hc)

Examines the differences between the U.S. and Japanese versions of over 50 different tokusatsu films like *Gojira* (1954)/*Godzilla, King of the Monsters!* (1956), *Gamera* (1965)/*Gammera, the Invincible* (1966), *Submersion of Japan* (1973)/*Tidal Wave* (1975), and many, many more! Softcover (540 pp./ 6"X9") Suggested Retail: $22.99 ISBN: 978-1-953221-77 -3

Examines the differences between the European and Japanese versions of tokusatsu films including the infamous "Cozzilla" colorized version of *Godzilla*, from 1977, plus rarities like *Terremoto 10 Grado*, the Italian cut of *Legend of Dinosaurs* and examines the condensed Champion Matsuri edits of Toho's effects films. Softcover (372 pp./ 6"X9") Suggested Retail: $19.99 ISBN: 978-1- 953221-77-3

Throughout the 1960s and 1970s the Italian film industry cranked out over 600 "Spaghetti Westerns" and for every *Fistful of Dollars* were a dozen pale imitations, some of them hilarious. Many of these lesser known Spaghettis are available in bargain bin DVD packs and stream for free online. If ever you've wondered which are worth this is the book for you. Softcover (160pp./5.06" X 7.8") Suggested Retail: $9.99

THE BICEP BOOKS CATALOGUE

CLASSIC MONSTERS SERIES

Kong Unmade explores unproduced scripts like *King Kong vs. Frankenstein* (1958), unfinished films like *The Lost Island* (1934), and lost movies like *King Kong Appears in Edo* (1938). As a bonus, all the Kong rip-offs like *Konga* (1961) and *Queen Kong* (1976) are reviewed. Hardcover (350 pp/5.83" X 8.27")/Softcover (376 pp/ 5.5" X 8.5") Suggested Retail: $24.99 (hc)/$19.99(sc) ISBN: 978-1-7341546-2-7(hc)

Jaws Unmade explores unproduced scripts like *Jaws 3, People 0* (1979), abandoned ideas like a Quint prequel, and even inspired movies like *Orca Part II*. As a bonus, all the Jaws rip-offs like *Grizzly* (1976) and *Tentacles* (1977) are reviewed. Hardcover (316 pp/5.83" X 8.27")/Softcover (340 pp/5.5" X 8.5") Suggested Retail: $29.99 (hc)/$17.95(sc) ISBN: 978-1-7344730-1-8

Classic Monsters Unmade covers lost and unmade films starring Dracula, Frankenstein, the Mummy and more monsters. Reviews unmade scripts like *The Return of Frankenstein* (1934) and *Wolf Man vs. Dracula* (1944). It also examines lost films of the silent era such as *The Werewolf* (1913) and *Drakula's Death* (1923). Softcover/ Hardcover(428pp/5.83"X8.27") Suggested Retail: $22.99(sc)/ $27.99(hc)ISBN:978-1-953221-85-8(hc)

Volume 2 explores the Hammer era and beyond, from unmade versions of *Brides of Dracula* (called *Disciple of Dracula*) to remakes of *Creature from the Black Lagoon*. Completely unmade films like *Kali: Devil Bride of Dracula* (1975) and *Godzilla vs. Frankenstein* (1964) are covered along with lost completed films like *Batman Fights Dracula* (1967) and *Black the Ripper* (1974). Coming Fall 2021.

NOSTALGIA

Written in the same spirit as *The Big Book of Japanese Giant Monster Movies*, this tome reviews all the classic Universal and Hammer horrors all the classic horrors that star Dracula, Frankenstein, the Gillman and the rest along with obscure flicks like *The New Invisible Man* (1958), *Billy the Kid versus Dracula* (1966), *Blackenstein* (1973) and *Legend of the Werewolf* (1974). Softcover (394 pp/5.5" X 8.5") Suggested Retail: $17.95

Written at an intermediate reading level for the kid in all of us, these picture books will take you back to your youth. In the spirit of the old Ian Thorne books are covered *Nabonga* (1944), *White Pongo* (1945) and more! Hardcover/Softcover (44 pp/7.5" X 9.25") Suggested Retail: $17.95(hc)/$9.99(sc) ISBN: 978- 1-7341546-9-6 (hc) 978- 1-7344730-5-6 (sc)

Written at an intermediate reading level for the kid in all of us, these picture books will take you back to your youth. In the spirit of the old Ian Thorne books are covered *The Lost World* (1925), *The Land That Time Forgot* (1975) and more! Hardcover/Softcover (44 pp/7.5" X 9.25") Suggested Retail: $17.95 (hc)/$9.99(sc) ISBN: 978-1-7344730 -6-3 (hc) 978-1-7344730-7-0 (sc)

Written at an intermediate reading level for the kid in all of us, these picture books will take you back to your youth. In the spirit of the old Ian Thorne books are covered *Them!* (1954), *Empire of the Ants* (1977) and more! Hardcover/ Softcover (44 pp/7.5" X 9.25") Suggested Retail: $17.95(hc)/ $9.99(sc) ISBN: 978-1-7347816 -3-2 (hc) 978 -1-7347816-2-5 (sc)

THE BICEP BOOKS CATALOGUE

CRYPTOZOOLOGY/COWBOYS & SAURIANS

Cowboys & Saurians: Prehistoric Beasts as Seen by the Pioneers explores dinosaur sightings from the pioneer period via real newspaper reports from the time. Well-known cases like the Tombstone Thunderbird are covered along with more obscure cases like the Crosswicks Monster and more. Softcover (357 pp/5.06" X 7.8") Suggested Retail: $19.95 ISBN: 978-1-7341546-1-0

Cowboys & Saurians: Ice Age zeroes in on snowbound saurians like the Ceratosaurus of the Arctic Circle and a Tyrannosaurus of the Tundra, as well as sightings of Ice Age megafauna like mammoths, glyptodonts, Sarkastodons and Saber-toothed tigers. Tales of a land that time forgot in the Arctic are also covered. Softcover (264 pp/5.06" X 7.8") Suggested Retail: $14.99 ISBN: 978-1-7341546-7-2

Southerners & Saurians takes the series formula of exploring newspaper accounts of monsters in the pioneer period with an eye to the Old South. In addition to dinosaurs are covered Lizardmen, Frogmen, giant leeches and mosquitoes, and the Dingocroc, which might be an alien rather than a prehistoric survivor. Softcover (202 pp/5.06" X 7.8") Suggested Retail: $13.99 ISBN: 978-1-7344730-4-9

Cowboys & Saurians South of the Border explores the saurians of Central and South America, like the Patagonian Plesiosaurus that was really an Iemisch, plus tales of the Neo-Mylodon, a menacing monster from underground called the Minhocao, Glyptodonts, and even Bolivia's three-headed dinosaur! Softcover (412 pp/5.06"X7.8") Suggested Retail: $17.95 ISBN: 978-1-953221-73-5

UFOLOGY/THE REAL COWBOYS & ALIENS IN CONJUNCTION WITH ROSWELL BOOKS

The Real Cowboys and Aliens: Early American UFOs explores UFO sightings in the USA between the years 1800-1864. Stories of encounters sometimes involved famous figures in U.S. history such as Lewis and Clark, and Thomas Jefferson. Hardcover (242pp/6" X 9") Softcover (262 pp/5.06" X 7.8") Suggested Retail: $24.99 (hc)/$15.95(sc) ISBN: 978-1-7341546-8-9\(hc)/978-1-7344 730-8-7(sc)

The second entry in the series, *Old West UFOs*, covers reports spanning the years 1865-1895. Includes tales of Men in Black, Reptilians, Spring-Heeled Jack, Sasquatch from space, and other alien beings, in addition to the UFOs and airships. Hardcover (276 pp/6" X 9") Softcover (308 pp/5.06" X 7.8") Suggested Retail: $29.95 (hc)/$17.95(sc) ISBN: 978-1-7344730-0-1 (hc)/ 978-1-73447 30-2-5 (sc)

The third entry in the series, *The Coming of the Airships*, encompasses a short time frame with an incredibly high concentration of airship sightings between 1896-1899. The famous Aurora, Texas, UFO crash of 1897 is covered in depth along with many others. Hardcover (196 pp/6" X 9") Softcover (222 pp/5.06" X 7.8") Suggested Retail: $24.99 (hc)/$15.95(sc) ISBN: 978-1-7347816 -1-8 (hc)/978-1-7347816-0-1(sc)

Early 20th Century UFOs kicks off a new series that investigates UFO sightings of the early 1900s. Includes tales of UFOs sighted over the *Titanic* as it sank, Nikola Tesla receiving messages from the stars, an alien being found encased in ice, and a possible virus from outer space! Hardcover (196 pp/6" X 9") Softcover (222 pp/5.06" X 9") Suggested Retail: $27.99 (hc)/$16.95(sc) ISBN: 978-1-7347816-1-8 (hc)/978-1-73478 16-0-1(sc)

LOST FILMS FANZINE BACK ISSUES

THE LOST FILMS FANZINE VOL.1

ISSUE #1 SPRING 2020 The lost Italian cut of *Legend of Dinosaurs and Monster Birds* called *Terremoto 10 Grado*, plus *Bride of Dr. Phibes* script, *Good Luck! Godzilla*, the King Kong remake that became a car comm ercial, Bollywood's lost *Jaws* rip-off, Top Ten Best Fan Made Godzilla trailers plus an interview with Scott David Lister. 60 pages. Three variant covers/editions (premium color/basic color/b&w)

ISSUE #2 SUMMER 2020 How 1935's *The Capture of Tarzan* became 1936's *Tarzan Escapes*, the Orca sequels that weren't, Baragon in Bollywood's *One Million B.C.*, unmade *Kolchak: The Night Stalker* movies, *The Norliss Tapes*, *Superman V: The New Movie*, why there were no *Curse of the Pink Panther* sequels, *Moonlight Mask: The Movie.* 64 pages. Two covers/editions (basic color/b&w)

ISSUE #3 FALL 2020 Blob sequels both forgotten and unproduced, *Horror of Dracula* uncut, *Franken-stein Meets the Wolfman* and talks, myths of the lost *King Kong* Spider-Pit sequence debunked, the *Carnosaur* novel vs. the movies, *Terror in the Streets* 50th anniversary, *Bride of Godzilla* 55th Unniversary, Lee Powers sketchbook. 100 pages. Two covers/editions (basic color/b&w)

ISSUE #4 WINTER 2020/21 *Diamonds Are Forever's* first draft with Goldfinger, *Disciple of Dracula* into *Brides of Dracula*, *War of the Worlds That Weren't* Part II, *Day the Earth Stood Still II* by Ray Bradbury, *Deathwish 6*, *Atomic War Bride*, *What Am I Doing in the Middle of a Revolution?*, *Spring Dream in the Old Capital* and more. 70 pages. Two covers/editions (basic color/b&w)

THE LOST FILMS FANZINE VOL.2

ISSUE #5 SPRING 2021 The lost films and projects of ape suit performer Charles Gemora, plus *Superman Reborn*, *Teenage Mutant Ninja Turtles IV: The Next Mutation*, *Mikado Zombie*, NBC's *Big Stuffed Dog*, King Ghidorah flies solo, *Grizzly II* reviewed, and War of the Worlds That Weren't concludes with a musical. Plus Blu-Ray reviews, news, and letters. 66 pages. Two covers/editions (basic co-lor/ b&w)

ISSUE #6 SUMMER 2021 Peter Sellers *Romance of the Pink Panther*, Akira Kurosawa's *Song of the Horse*, *Kali - Devil Bride of Dracula*, Jack Black as Green Lantern, *Ladybug, Ladybug*, *The Lost Atlantis*, Japan's lost superhero Hiyo Man, and *Lord of Light*, the CIA's covert movie that inspired 2012's *Argo*. Plus news, Blu-Ray reviews, and letters. 72 pages. Two covers/editions (basic color/b&w)

ISSUE #7 FALL 2021 *Hiero's Journey*, Don Bragg in *Tarzan and the Jewels of Opar*, DC's *Lobo* movie, Lee Powers Scrapbook returns, Blake Matthews uncovers *The Big Boss Part II* (1976), Matthew B. Lamont searches for lost Three Stooges, and an ape called Kong in 1927's *Isle of Sunken Gold.* Plus news, and letters. 72 pages. Two covers/editions (basic color /b&w)

ISSUE #8 WINTER 2021/22 The connection between Steve Reeves' unmade third Hercules movie and *Goliath and the Dragon*, *The Iron Man* starring Tom Cruise, Phil Yordan's *King Kong* remake, *The Unearthly Stranger*, *Saturday Super-cade* forgotten cartoon, the 45th anniversary of Luigi Cozzi's "Cozzila" and *Day the Earth Froze.* Plus news and letters. 72 pages. Two covers/editions (basic color /b&w)

MOVIE MILESTONES BACK ISSUES

MOVIE MILESTONES VOL. 1   VOL. 2

ISSUE #1 AUGUST 2020 Debut issue celebrating 80 years of *One Million B.C.* (1940), and an early 55th Anniversary for *One Million Years B.C.* (1966). Abandoned ideas, casting changes, and deleted scenes are covered, plus a mini-B.C. stock-footage filmography and much more! 54 pages. Three collectible covers/ editions (premium color/ basic color/b&w)

ISSUE #2 OCTOBER 2020 Celebrates the joint 50th Anniversaries of *When Dinosaurs Ruled the Earth* (1970) and *Creatures the World Forgot* (1971). Also includes looks at *Prehistoric Women* (1967), *When Women Had Tails* (1970), and *Caveman* (1981), plus unmade films like *When the World Cracked Open.* 72 pages. Three collectible covers/editions (premium color/basic color/b&w)

ISSUE #3 WINTER 2021 Japanese 'Panic Movies' like *The Last War* (1961), *Submersion of Japan* (1973), and *Bullet Train* (1975) are covered on celebrated author Sakyo Komatsu's 90th birthday. The famous banned Toho film *Prophecies of Nostradamus* (1974) are also covered. 124 pages. Three collectible covers/ editions (premium color/ basic color/ b&w)

ISSUE #4 SPRING 2021 This issue celebrates the joint 60th Anniversaries of *Gorgo, Reptilicus* and *Konga* examining unmade sequels like *Reptilicus 2*, and other related lost projects like *Kuru Island* and *The Volcano Monsters.* Also explores the Gorgo, Konga and Reptilicus comic books from Charlton. 72 pages. Three collectible covers/editions (premium color/basic color/b&w)

MOVIE MILESTONES VOL. 2   VOL. 3 COMING SOON

ISSUE #5 SUMMER 2021 *Godzilla vs. the Sea Monster* gets the spotlight, with an emphasis on its original version *King Kong vs. Ebirah*, plus information on *The King Kong Show* which inspired it, and Jun Fukuda's tangentially related spy series *100 Shot/100 Killed.* 72 pages. Three collectible covers/editions (premium color /basic color/b&w)

ISSUE #6 FALL 2021 Monster Westerns of the 1950s and 1960s are spotlighted in the form of *Teenage Monster, The Curse of the Undead, Billy the Kid Versus Dracula, Jesse James Meets Frankenstein's Daughter*, and Bela Lugosi's unmade *The Ghoul Goes West.* 50 pages. Special Black and White exclusive!

ISSUE #7 WINTER 2022 This issue is all about Amicus's Edgar Rice Burroughs trilogy including *Land That Time Forgot, At the Earth's Core, People That Time Forgot* plus unmade sequels like Out of Time's Abyss or Doug McClure as John Carter of Mars. All this plus *Warlords of Atlantis* and *Arabian Adventure!* 100 pages. Three collectible covers/editions (premium color /basic color/b&w)

ISSUE #8 SPRING 2022 *Godzilla vs. Gigan* turns 50 and this issue is here to celebrate with its many unmade versions, like *Godzilla vs. the Space Monsters* and *Return of King Ghidorah*, plus *The Mysterians* 65th anniversary and *Daigoro vs. Goliath's* 50th.

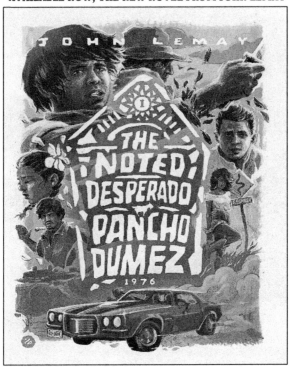

Twenty-six years ago, outlaw Billy the Kid's tombstone was stolen from Fort Sumner, New Mexico. Now it has mysteriously been returned. When teenage brothers Pancho and Dorado Dumez steal it themselves, they get more than they bargained for. Encased inside the tombstone is a map that leads to the Southwest's greatest treasure: The Lost Adams Diggings—a canyon comprised of solid gold. But the brothers aren't the only ones on the treasure's trail. So is bounty hunter Seven McCaw, and along with him comes a modern-day incarnation of the Santa Fe Ring—a secretive organization that once ruled the West. Forced onto the open roads of New Mexico, the brothers must solve the mystery of Billy the Kid's death and find the lost canyon before the Ring does...

Printed in Great Britain
by Amazon

24967126R00110